PHILIP RAHV, Visiting Professor of Comparative Literature
at Brandeis University and a Senior Fellow of the School
of English of the University of Indiana, was born in
Russia and came to this country at the age of thirteen; he
was educated in this country and in Europe. He has been
an editor of *Partisan Review,* one of America's leading
cultural reviews, since its foundation in 1934. Among the
books he has edited are *Discovery of Europe: The Story
of American Experience in the Old World, The Great
Short Novels of Henry James, The Short Novels of Leo
Tolstoy, The Partisan Reader: Ten Years of Partisan Review* (with William Phillips), and *Literature in America.*

IMAGE AND IDEA

IMAGE AND IDEA

Twenty Essays on Literary

Themes by PHILIP RAHV

REVISED AND ENLARGED

A New Directions Paperbook

Manufactured in the United States of America.
New Directions Books are published at Norfolk, Connecticut
by James Laughlin. New York office—333 Sixth Avenue (14).
Design by Stefan Salter

TO NATHALIE

FOREWORD

This new edition of *Image and Idea* differs from the original edition of 1949 in that it has been considerably revised and enlarged. The essay on "Dostoevsky in *The Possessed*" and a wartime polemic against the late Bernard de Voto, which is only of slight interest today, have been omitted, while eight pieces, heretofore uncollected in book form, have been added. The additions consist of the essay "An Introduction to Kafka" and the last seven pieces in the section entitled "Sketches in Criticism." This section, because of the topical references that now and then occur in it, has been arranged in chronological order, with the dates of composition appended.

It is perhaps worth noting that the two essays on James were written before the revival of this classic American novelist, a revival long in preparation, which was finally brought to a head, in the fall of 1944, by the simultaneous appearance of two anthologies of his fiction. As the editor of one of those anthologies I was quite as surprised as anyone else by the unexpected dimensions of the interest in him and by the collapse of the resistance to his appeal in some of the literary and academic circles characterized in the shorter essay on James in this volume. But it may well be that his apotheosis is not quite what was wanted.

For it seems that the long-standing prejudice against him has now given way to an uncritical adulation which, in a different way, is perhaps quite as retarding to a sound appraisal of his achievement.

With the exception of the piece on Gogol, all the essays included in this edition first appeared in periodicals: a good many in *Partisan Review*, others in *The Southern Review*, *The Kenyon Review*, *The Nation*, *The New Republic*, *The New Leader*, and *Commentary*. To those magazines my thanks and acknowledgments are due.

P. R.

CONTENTS

PALEFACE AND REDSKIN

Viewed historically, American writers appear to group
themselves around two polar types. Paleface and redskin
I should like to call the two, and despite occasional efforts
at reconciliation no love is lost between them.

Consider the immense contrast between the drawing-
room fictions of Henry James and the open air poems of
Walt Whitman. Compare Melville's decades of loneliness,
his tragic failure, with Mark Twain's boisterous career
and dubious success. At one pole there is the literature
of the lowlife world of the frontier and of the big cities; at
the other the thin, solemn, semi-clerical culture of Boston
and Concord. The fact is that the creative mind in America is fragmented and one-sided. For the process of polarization has produced a dichotomy between experience and
consciousness—a dissociation between energy and sensibility, between conduct and theories of conduct, between
life conceived as an opportunity and life conceived as a
discipline.

The differences between the two types define themselves in every sphere. Thus while the redskin glories in
his Americanism, to the paleface it is a source of endless
ambiguities. Sociologically they can be distinguished as
patrician vs. plebeian, and in their aesthetic ideals one

is drawn to allegory and the distillations of symbolism, whereas the other inclines to a gross, riotous naturalism. The paleface is a "high-brow," though his mentality—as in the case of Hawthorne and James—is often of the kind that excludes and repels general ideas; he is at the same time both something more and something less than an intellectual in the European sense. And the redskin deserves the epithet "low-brow," not because he is badly educated—which he might or might not be—but because his reactions are primarily emotional, spontaneous, and lacking in personal culture. The paleface continually hankers after religious norms, tending toward a refined estrangement from reality. The redskin, on the other hand, accepts his environment, at times to the degree of fusion with it, even when rebelling against one or another of its manifestations. At his highest level the paleface moves in an exquisite moral atmosphere; at his lowest he is genteel, snobbish, and pedantic. In giving expression to the vitality and to the aspirations of the people, the redskin is at his best; but at his worst he is a vulgar anti-intellectual, combining aggression with conformity and reverting to the crudest forms of frontier psychology.

James and Whitman, who as contemporaries felt little more than contempt for each other, are the purest examples of this dissociation.* In reviewing *Drum Taps* in 1865 the young James told off the grand plebeian innovator, advising him to stop declaiming and go sit in the corner of a rhyme and meter school, while the innovator, snorting at the novelist of scruples and moral delicacy, said "Feathers!" Now this mutual repulsion between the two major figures in American literature would be less important if it were mainly personal or aesthetic in reference. But the point is that it has a profoundly national and social-historical character.

* According to Edith Wharton, James changed his mind about Whitman late in life. But this can be regarded as a private fact of the Jamesian sensibility, for in public he said not a word in favor of Whitman.

James and Whitman form a kind of fatal antipodes. To this, in part, can be traced the curious fact about them that, though each has become the object of a special cult, neither is quite secure in his reputation. For most of the critics and historians who make much of Whitman disparage James or ignore him altogether, and vice versa. Evidently the high valuation of the one is so incongruous with the high valuation of the other that criticism is chronically forced to choose between them—which makes for a breach in the literary tradition without parallel in any European country. The aristocrat Tolstoy and the tramp Gorky found that they held certain values and ideas in common, whereas James and Whitman, who between them dominate American writing of the nineteenth century, cannot abide with one another. And theirs is no unique or isolated instance.

The national literature suffers from the ills of a split personality. The typical American writer has so far shown himself incapable of escaping the blight of one-sidedness: of achieving that mature control which permits the balance of impulse with sensitiveness, of natural power with philosophical depth. For the dissociation of mind from experience has resulted in truncated works of art, works that tend to be either naive and ungraded, often flat reproductions of life, or else products of cultivation that remain abstract because they fall short on evidence drawn from the sensuous and material world. Hence it is only through intensively exploiting their very limitations, through submitting themselves to a process of creative yet cruel self-exaggeration, that a few artists have succeeded in warding off the failure that threatened them. And the later novels of Henry James are a case in point.

The palefaces dominated literature throughout the nineteenth century, but in the twentieth they were overthrown by the redskins. Once the continent had been mastered, with the plebeian bourgeoisie coming into complete possession of the national wealth, and puritanism had worn itself out, degenerating into mere respectability,

3

it became objectively possible and socially permissible to satisfy that desire for experience and personal emancipation which heretofore had been systematically frustrated. The era of economic accumulation had ended and the era of consummation had arrived. To enjoy life now became one of the functions of progress—a function for which the palefaces were temperamentally disqualified. This gave Mencken his opportunity to emerge as the ideologue of enjoyment. Novelists like Dreiser, Anderson, and Lewis—and, in fact, most of the writers of the period of "experiment and liberation"—rose against conventions that society itself was beginning to abandon. They helped to "liquidate" the lag between the enormous riches of the nation and its morality of abstention. The neo-humanists were among the last of the breed of palefaces, and they perished in the quixotic attempt to re-establish the old values. Eliot forsook his native land, while the few palefaces who managed to survive at home took to the academic or else to the "higher" and relatively unpopular forms of writing. But the novelists, who control the main highway of literature, were, and still are, nearly all redskins to the wigwam born.

At present the redskins are in command of the situation, and the literary life in America has seldom been so deficient in intellectual power. The political interests introduced in the nineteen-thirties have not only strengthened their hold but have also brought out their worst tendencies; for the effect of the popular political creeds of our time has been to increase their habitual hostility to ideas, sanctioning the relaxation of standards and justifying the urge to come to terms with semi-literate audiences.

The redskin writer in America is a purely indigenous phenomenon, the true-blue offspring of the western hemisphere, the juvenile in principle and for the good of the soul. He is a self-made writer in the same way that Henry Ford was a self-made millionaire. On the one hand he is a crass materialist, a greedy consumer of experience, and on the other a sentimentalist, a half-baked mystic listening to inward voices and watching for signs and portents. Think of Dreiser, Lewis, Anderson, Wolfe, Sandburg, Caldwell, Steinbeck, Farrell, Saroyan: all writers of genuine and some even of admirable accomplishments, whose faults, however, are not so much literary as faults of raw life itself. Unable to relate himself in any significant manner to the cultural heritage, the redskin writer is always on his own; and since his personality resists growth and change, he must continually repeat himself. His work is ridden by compulsions that depress the literary tradition, because they are compulsions of a kind that put a strain on literature, that literature more often than not can neither assimilate nor sublimate. He is the passive instead of the active agent of the *Zeitgeist*, he lives off it rather than through it, so that when his particular gifts happen to coincide with the mood of the times he seems modern and contemporary, but once the mood has passed he is in danger of being quickly discarded. Lacking the qualities of surprise and renewal, already Dreiser and Anderson, for example, have a "period" air about them that makes a re-reading of their work something of a critical chore; and one suspects that Hemingway, that perennial boy-man, is more accurately understood as a descendant of Natty Bumppo, the hero of Fenimore Cooper's Leather-stocking tales, than as the portentously disillusioned character his legend makes him out to be.

As for the paleface, in compensation for backward cultural conditions and a lost religious ethic, he has developed a supreme talent for refinement, just as the Jew, in compensation for adverse social conditions and a lost national independence, has developed a supreme talent for cleverness. (In this connection it is pertinent to recall T. S. Eliot's remark about Boston society, which he described as "quite refined, but refined beyond the point of civilization.") Now this peculiar excess of refinement is to be deplored in an imaginative writer, for it weakens his capacity to cope with experience and induces in him a fetishistic attitude toward tradition; nor is this species of

5

refinement to be equated with the refinement of artists like Proust or Mann, as in them it is not an element contradicting an open and bold confrontation of reality. Yet the paleface, being above all a conscious individual, was frequently able to transcend or to deviate sharply from the norms of his group, and he is to be credited with most of the rigors and charms of the classic American books. While it is true, as John Jay Chapman put it, that his culture is "secondary and tertiary" and that between him and the sky "float the Constitution of the United States and the traditions and forms of English literature"—nevertheless, there exists the poetry of Emily Dickinson, there is *The Scarlet Letter,* there is *Moby Dick,* and there are not a few incomparable narratives by Henry James.

At this point there is no necessity to enter into a discussion of the historical and social causes that account for the disunity of the American creative mind. In various contexts a number of critics have disclosed and evaluated the forces that have worked on this mind and shaped it to their uses. The sole question that seems relevant is whether history will make whole again what it has rent asunder. Will James and Whitman ever be reconciled, will they finally discover and act upon each other? Only history can give a definite reply to this question. In the meantime, however, there are available the resources of effort and understanding, resources which even those who believe in the strict determination of the cultural object need not spurn.

THE CULT OF EXPERIENCE
IN AMERICAN WRITING

Every attentive reader of Henry James remembers that
highly dramatic scene in *The Ambassadors*—a scene
singled out by its author as giving away the "whole case"
of his novel—in which Lambert Strether, the elderly New
England gentleman who had come to Paris on a mission
of business and duty, proclaims his conversion to the
doctrine of experience. Caught in the spell of Paris, the
discovery of whose grace and form is marked for him by a
kind of meaning and intensity that can be likened only to
the raptures of a mystic vision, Strether feels moved to
renounce publicly the morality of abstention he had
brought with him from Woollett, Mass. And that mellow
Sunday afternoon, as he mingles with the charming
guests assembled in the garden of the sculptor Gloriani,
the spell of the world capital of civilization is so strong
upon the sensitive old man that he trembles with happiness and zeal. It is then that he communicates to little
Bilham his newly acquired piety toward life and the
fruits thereof. The worst mistake one can make, he ad-
monishes his youthful interlocutor, is not to live all one
can.—"Do what you like so long as you don't make my
mistake . . . Live! . . . It doesn't so much matter what
you do in particular, so long as you have your life. If you

haven't had that, what *have* you had? . . . This place and these impressions . . . have had their abundant message for me, have just dropped *that* into my mind. I see it now . . . and more than you'd believe or I can express. . . . The right time is now yours. The right time is any *time* that one is still so lucky as to have . . . Live, Live!"

To an imaginative European, unfamiliar with the prohibitive American past and the long-standing national habit of playing hide and seek with experience, Strether's pronouncements in favor of sheer life may well seem so commonplace as scarcely to be worth the loving concentration of a major novelist. While the idea that one should "live" one's life came to James as a revelation, to the contemporary European writers this idea had long been a thoroughly assimilated and natural assumption. Experience served them as the concrete medium for the testing and creation of values, whereas in James's work it stands for something distilled or selected from the total process of living; it stands for romance, reality, civilization—a self-propelling, autonomous "presence" inexhaustibly alluring in its own right. That is the "presence" which in the imagination of Hyacinth Robinson, the hero of *The Princess Casamassima,* takes on a form at once "vast, vague, and dazzling—an irradiation of light from objects undefined, mixed with the atmosphere of Paris and Venice."

The significance of this positive approach to experience and identification of it with life's "treasures, felicities, splendors and successes" is that it represents a momentous break with the then dominant American morality of abstention. The roots of this morality are to be traced on the one hand to the religion of the Puritans and, on the other, to the inescapable need of a frontier society to master its world in sober practice before appropriating it as an object of enjoyment. Such is the historical content of that native "innocence" which in James's fiction is continually being ensnared in the web of European "experience." And James's tendency is to resolve this drama of entanglement by finally accepting what Europe offers on condition that it cleanse itself of its taint of evil through an alliance with New World virtue.

James's attitude toward experience is sometimes overlooked by readers excessively impressed (or depressed) by his oblique methods and effects of remoteness and ambiguity. Actually, from the standpoint of the history of the national letters, the lesson he taught in *The Ambassadors,* as in many of his other works, must be understood as no less than a revolutionary appeal. It is a veritable declaration of the rights of man—not, to be sure, of the rights of the public, of the social man, but of the rights of the private man, of the rights of personality, whose openness to experience provides the sole effective guaranty of its development. Already in one of his earliest stories we find the observation that "in this country the people have rights but the person has none." And in so far as any artist can be said to have had a mission, his manifestly was to brace the American individual in his moral struggle to gain for his personal and subjective life that measure of freedom which, as a citizen of a prosperous and democratic community, he had long been enjoying in the sphere of material and political relations.

Strether's appeal, in curiously elaborated, varied, as well as ambivalent forms, pervades all of James's work; and for purposes of critical symbolization it might well be regarded as the compositional key to the whole modern movement in American writing. No literature, it might be said, takes on the qualities of a truly national body of expression unless it is possessed by a basic theme and unifying principle of its own. Thus the German creative mind has in the main been actuated by philosophical interests, the French by the highest ambitions of the intelligence unrestrained by system or dogma, the Russian by the passionately candid questioning and shaping of values. And since Whitman and James the American creative mind, seizing at last upon what had long been denied to

9

it, has found the terms and objects of its activity in the urge toward and immersion in experience. It is this search for experience, conducted on diverse and often conflicting levels of consciousness, which has been the dominant, quintessential theme of the characteristic American literary productions—from *Leaves of Grass* to *Winesburg, Ohio* and beyond; and the more typically American the writer —a figure like Thomas Wolfe is a patent example—the more deeply does it engulf him.

It is through this preoccupation, it seems to me, that one can account, perhaps more adequately than through any other factor, for some of the peculiarities of American writing since the close of its classic period. A basis is thus provided for explaining the unique indifference of this literature to certain cultural aims implicit in the aesthetic rendering of experience—to ideas generally, to theories of value, to the wit of the speculative and problematical, and to that new-fashioned sense of irony which at once expresses and modulates the conflicts in modern belief. In his own way even a writer as intensely aware as James shares this indifference. He is the analyst of fine consciences, and fine minds too, but scarcely of minds capable of grasping and acting upon those ineluctable problems that enter so prominently and with such significant results into the literary art developed in Europe during the past hundred years. And the question is not whether James belonged among the "great thinkers"— very few novelists do—but whether he is "obsessed" by those universal problems, whether, in other words, his work is vitally associated with that prolonged crisis of the human spirit to which the concept of modernity is ultimately reducible. What James asks for, primarily, is the expansion of life beyond its primitive needs and elementary standards of moral and material utility; and of culture he conceives as the reward of this expansion and as its unfailing means of discrimination. Hence he searches for the whereabouts of "Life" and for the exact conditions of its enrichment. This is what makes for a fundamental

10

difference between the inner movement of the American and that of the European novel, the novel of Tolstoy and Dostoevsky, Flaubert and Proust, Joyce, Mann, Lawrence, and Kafka, whose problem is invariably posed in terms of life's intrinsic worth and destiny.

The intellectual is the only character missing in the American novel. He may appear in it in his professional capacity—as artist, teacher, or scientist—but very rarely as a person who thinks with his entire being, that is to say, as a person who transforms ideas into actual dramatic motives instead of merely using them as ideological conventions or as theories so externally applied that they can be dispensed with at will. Everything is contained in the American novel except ideas. But what are ideas? At best judgments of reality and at worst substitutes for it. The American novelist's conversion to reality, however, has been so belated that he cannot but be baffled by judgments and vexed by substitutes. Thus his work exhibits a singular pattern consisting, on the one hand, of a disinclination to thought and, on the other, of an intense predilection for the real: and the real appears in it as a vast phenomenology swept by waves of sensation and feeling. In this welter there is little room for the intellect, which in the unconscious belief of many imaginative Americans is naturally impervious, if not wholly inimical, to reality.

Consider the literary qualities of Ernest Hemingway, for example. There is nothing Hemingway dislikes more than experience of a make-believe, vague, or frigid nature, but in order to safeguard himself against the counterfeit he consistently avoids drawing upon the more abstract resources of the mind, he snubs the thinking man and mostly confines himself to the depiction of life on its physical levels. Of course, his rare mastery of the sensuous element largely compensates for whatever losses he may sustain in other spheres. Yet the fact remains that a good part of his writing leaves us with a sense of situations unresolved and with a picture of human beings tested by values much too simplified to do them justice. Cleanth

11

Brooks and Robert Penn Warren have recently remarked on the interrelation between qualities of Hemingway's style and his bedazzlement by sheer experience. The following observation in particular tends to bear out the point of view expressed in this essay: "The short simple rhythms, the succession of coordinate clauses, the general lack of subordination—all suggest a dislocated and un-unified world. The figures which live in this world live a sort of hand-to-mouth existence perceptually, and conceptually, they hardly live at all. Subordination implies some exercise of discrimination—the sifting of reality through the intellect. But Hemingway has a romantic anti-intellectualism which is to be associated with the premium which he places upon experience as such."[*]

But Hemingway is only a specific instance. Other writers, less gifted and not so self-sufficiently and incisively one-sided, have come to grief through this same creative psychology. Under its conditioning some of them have produced work so limited to the recording of the unmistakably and recurrently real that it can truly be said of them that their art ends exactly where it should properly begin.

"How can one make the best of one's life?" André Malraux asks in one of his novels. "By converting as wide a range of experience as possible into conscious thought." It is precisely this reply which is alien to the typical American artist, who all too often is so absorbed in experience that he is satisfied to let it "write its own ticket"—to carry him, that is, to its own chance or casual destination.

In the first part of *Faust* Goethe removes his hero, a Gothic dreamer, from the cell of scholastic devotion in order to embroil him in the passions and high-flavored joys of "real life." But in the second part of the play this hero attains a broader stage of consciousness, reconciling the perilous freedom of his newly released personality with the enduring interests of the race, with high art,

_____
[*] Cf. "The Killers," by Cleanth Brooks and Robert Penn Warren, in *American Prefaces*, Spring 1942.

politics, and the constructive labor of curbing the chaotic forces in man and nature alike. This progress of Faust is foreshadowed in an early scene, when Mephisto promises to reveal to him "the little and then the great world."— *Wir sehen die kleine, dann die grosse Welt.*—The little world is the world of the individual bemused by his personal experience, and his sufferings, guilt-feelings, and isolation are to be understood as the penalty he pays for throwing off the traditional bonds that once linked him to God and his fellow-men. Beyond the little world, however, lies the broader world of man the inhabitant of his own history, who in truth is always losing his soul in order to gain it. Now the American drama of experience constitutes a kind of half-*Faust*, a play with the first part intact and the second part missing. And the Mephisto of this shortened version is the familiar demon of the Puritan morality-play, not at all the Goethian philosopher-sceptic driven by the nihilistic spirit of the modern epoch. Nor is the plot of this half-*Faust* consistent within itself. For its protagonist, playing Gretchen as often as he plays Faust, is evidently unclear in his own mind as to the role he is cast in—that of the seducer or the seduced?

It may be that this confusion of roles is the inner source of the famous Jamesian ambiguity and ever-recurring theme of betrayal. James's heroines—his Isabel Archers and Milly Theales and Maggie Ververs—are they not somehow always being victimized by the "great world" even as they succeed in mastering it? Gretchen-like in their innocence, they none the less enact the Faustian role in their uninterrupted pursuit of experience and in the use of the truly Mephistophelean gold of their millionaire-fathers to buy up the brains and beauty and nobility of the civilization that enchants them. And the later heroes of American fiction—Hemingway's young man, for instance, who invariably appears in each of his novels, a young man posing his virility against the background of continents and nations so old that, like Tiresias, they have seen all and suffered all—in his own way he, too, responds to experience in the schizoid fashion of the Gretchen-Faust character. For what is his virility if not at once the measure of his innocence and the measure of his aggression? And what shall we make of Steinbeck's fable of Lennie, that mindless giant who literally kills and gets killed from sheer desire for those soft and lovely things of which fate has singularly deprived him? He combines an unspeakable innocence with an unspeakable aggression. Perhaps it is not too far-fetched to say that in this grotesque creature Steinbeck has unconsciously created a symbolic parody of a figure such as Thomas Wolfe, who likewise crushed in his huge caresses the delicate objects of the art of life.

The disunity of American literature, its polar division into above and below or paleface and redskin writing, I have noted elsewhere. Whitman and James, who form a kind of fatal antipodes, have served as the standard examples of this dissociation. There is one sense, however, in which the contrast between these two archetypal Americans may be said to have been overdrawn. There is, after all, a common ground on which they finally, though perhaps briefly, meet—an essential Americanism subsuming them both that is best defined by their mutual affirmation of experience. True, what one affirmed the other was apt to negate; still it is not in their attitudes toward experience as such that the difference between them becomes crucial but rather in their contradictory conceptions of what constitutes experience. One sought its ideal manifestations in America, the other in Europe. Whitman, plunging with characteristic impetuosity into the turbulent, formless life of the frontier and the big cities, accepted experience in its total ungraded state, whereas James, insisting on a precise scrutiny of its origins and conditions, was endlessly discriminatory, thus carrying forward his ascetic inheritance into the very act of reaching out for the charms and felicities of the great European world. But the important thing to keep in mind here is that this

14

plebeian and patrician are historically associated, each in his own incomparable way, in the radical enterprise of subverting the puritan code of stark utility in the conduct of life and in releasing the long compressed springs of experience in the national letters. In this sense, Whitman and James are the true initiators of the American line of modernity.

If a positive approach to experience is the touchstone of the modern, a negative approach is the touchstone of the classic in American writing. The literature of early America is a sacred rather than a profane literature. Immaculately spiritual at the top and local and anecdotal at the bottom, it is essentially, as the genteel literary historian Barrett Wendell accurately noted, a "record of the national inexperience" marked by "instinctive disregard of actual fact." For this reason it largely left untouched the two chief experiential media—the novel and the drama. Brockden Brown, Cooper, Hawthorne, and Melville were "romancers" and poets rather than novelists. They were incapable of apprehending the vitally new principle of realism by virtue of which the art of fiction in Europe was in their time rapidly evolving toward a hitherto inconceivable condition of objectivity and familiarity with existence. Not until James did a fiction-writer appear in America who was able to sympathize with and hence to take advantage of the methods of George Eliot, Balzac, and Turgenev. Since the principle of realism presupposes a thoroughly secularized relationship between the ego and experience, Hawthorne and Melville could not possibly have apprehended it. Though not religious men themselves, they were nevertheless held in bondage by ancestral conscience and dogma, they were still living in the afterglow of a religious faith that drove the ego, on its external side, to aggrandize itself by accumulating practical sanctions while scourging and inhibiting its intimate side. In Hawthorne the absent or suppressed experience reappears in the shape of spectral beings whose function is to warn, repel, and fascinate.

And the unutterable confusion that reigns in some of Melville's narratives (*Pierre, Mardi*) is primarily due to his inability either to come to terms with experience or else wholly and finally to reject it.

Despite the featureless innocence and moral enthusiastic air of the old American books, there is in some of them a peculiar virulence, a feeling of discord that does not easily fit in with the general tone of the classic age. In such worthies as Irving, Cooper, Bryant, Longfellow, Whittier, and Lowell there is scarcely anything more than meets the eye, but in Poe, Hawthorne, and Melville there is an incandescent symbolism, a meaning within meaning, the vitality of which is perhaps only now being rightly appreciated. D. H. Lawrence was close to the truth when he spoke of what serpents they were, of the "inner diabolism of their underconsciousness." Hawthorne, "that blue-eyed darling," as well as Poe and Melville, insisted on a subversive vision of human nature at the same time as cultivated Americans were everywhere relishing the orations of Emerson who, as James put it, was helping them "to take a picturesque view of one's internal possibilities and to find in the landscape of the soul all sorts of fine sunrise and moonlight effects." Each of these three creative men displays a healthy resistance to the sentimentality and vague idealism of his contemporaries; and along with this resistance they display morbid qualities that, aside from any specific biographical factors, might perhaps be accounted for by the contradiction between the poverty of the experience provided by the society they lived in and the high development of their moral, intellectual, and affective natures—though in Poe's case there is no need to put any stress on his moral character. And the curious thing is that whatever faults their work shows are reversed in later American literature, the weaknesses of which are not to be traced to poverty of experience but to an inability to encompass it on a significant level.

The dilemma that confronted these early writers chiefly

16

manifests itself in their frequent failure to integrate the inner and outer elements of their world so that they might stand witness for each other by way of the organic linkage of object and symbol, act and meaning. For that is the linkage of art without which its structure cannot stand. Lawrence thought that *Moby Dick* is profound *beyond* human feeling—which in a sense says as much against the book as for it. Its further defects are dispersion, a divided mind: its real and transcendental elements do not fully interpenetrate, the creative tension between them is more fortuitous than organic. In *The Scarlet Letter* as in a few of his shorter fictions, and to a lesser degree in *The Blithedale Romance,* Hawthorne was able to achieve an imaginative order that otherwise eluded him. A good deal of his writing, despite his gift for precise observation, consists of phantasy unsupported by the conviction of reality.

Many changes had to take place in America before its spiritual and material levels could fuse in a work of art in a more or less satisfactory manner. Whitman was already in the position to vivify his democratic ethos by an appeal to the physical features of the country, such as the grandeur and variety of its geography, and to the infinite detail of common lives and occupations. And James too, though sometimes forced to resort to makeshift situations, was on the whole successful in setting up a lively and significant exchange between the moral and empiric elements of his subject-matter. Though he was, in a sense, implicitly bound all his life by the morality of Hawthorne, James none the less perceived what the guilt-tossed psyche of the author of *The Marble Faun* prevented him from seeing—that it is not the man trusting himself to experience but the one fleeing from it who suffers the "beast in the jungle" to rend him.

The Transcendentalist movement is peculiar in that it expresses the native tradition of inexperience in its particulars and the revolutionary urge to experience in its generalities. (Perhaps that is what Van Wyck Brooks meant when, long before prostrating himself at his shrine, he wrote that Emerson was habitually abstract where he should be concrete, and vice versa.) On a purely theoretical plane, in ways curiously inverted and idealistic, the cult of experience is patently prefigured in Emerson's doctrine of the uniqueness and infinitude, as well as in Thoreau's equally steep estimate, of the private man. American culture was then unprepared for anything more drastic than an affirmation of experience in theory alone, and even the theory was modulated in a semiclerical fashion so as not to set it in too open an opposition to the dogmatic faith that, despite the decay of its theology, still prevailed in the ethical sphere. "The love which is preached nowadays," wrote Thoreau, "is an ocean of new milk for a man to swim in. I hear no surf nor surge, but the winds coo over it." No wonder, then, that Transcendentalism declared itself most clearly and dramatically in the form of the essay—a form in which one can preach without practicing.

Personal liberation from social taboos and conventions was the war cry of the group of writers that came to the fore in the second decade of the century. They employed a variety of means to formulate and press home this program. Dreiser's tough-minded though somewhat arid naturalism, Anderson's softer and spottier method articulating the protest of shut-in people, Lewis's satires of Main Street, Cabell's florid celebrations of pleasure, Edna Millay's emotional expansiveness, Mencken's worldly wisdom and assaults on the provincial pieties, the early Van Wyck Brook's high-minded though bitter evocations of the inhibited past, his ideal of creative self-fulfillment—all these were weapons brought to bear by the party of rebellion in the struggle to gain free access to experience. And the secret of energy in that struggle seems to have been the longing for what was then called "sexual freedom"; for at the time Americans seeking emancipation were engaged in a truly elemental discovery of sex whose literary

18

expression on some levels, as Randolph Bourne remarked, easily turned into "caricatures of desire." The novel, the poem, the play—all contributed to the development of a complete symptomatology of sexual frustration and release. In his *Memoirs,* written toward the end of his life, Sherwood Anderson recalled the writers of that period as "a little band of soldiers who were going to free life . . . from certain bonds." Not that they wanted to overplay sex, but they did want "to bring it back into real relation to the life we lived and saw others living. We wanted the flesh back in our literature, wanted directly in our literature the fact of men and women in bed together, babies being born. We wanted the terrible importance of the flesh in human relations also revealed again." In retrospect much of this writing seems but a naive inversion of the dear old American innocence, a turning inside out of inbred fear and reticence, but the qualities one likes in it are its positiveness of statement, its zeal and pathos of the limited view.

The concept of experience was then still an undifferentiated whole. But as the desire for personal liberation, even if only from the less compulsive social pressures, was partly gratified and the tone of the literary revival changed from eagerness to disdain, the sense of totality gradually wore itself out. Since the nineteen-twenties a process of atomization of experience has forced each of its spokesmen into a separate groove from which he can step out only at the risk of utterly disorienting himself. Thus, to cite some random examples, poetic technique became the special experience of Ezra Pound, language that of Gertrude Stein, the concrete object was appropriated by W. C. Williams, super-American phenomena by Sandburg and related nationalists, Kenneth Burke experienced ideas (which is by no means the same as thinking them), Archibald MacLeish experienced public attitudes, F. Scott Fitzgerald the glamor and sadness of the very rich, Hemingway death and virile sports, and so on and so forth. Finally Thomas Wolfe plunged into a chaotic recapitulation of the cult of experience as a whole, traversing it in all directions and ending nowhere.

Though the crisis of the nineteen-thirties arrested somewhat the progress of the experiential mode, it nevertheless managed to put its stamp on the entire social-revolutionary literature of the decade. A comparison of European and American left-wing writing of the same period will at once show that whereas Europeans like Malraux and Silone enter deeply into the meaning of political ideas and beliefs, Americans touch only superficially on such matters, as actually their interest is fixed almost exclusively on the class war as an experience which, to them at least, is new and exciting. They succeed in representing incidents of oppression and revolt, as well as sentimental conversions, but conversions of the heart and mind they merely sketch in on the surface or imply in a gratuitous fashion. (What does a radical novel like *The Grapes of Wrath* contain, from an ideological point of view, that agitational journalism cannot communicate with equal heat and facility. Surely its vogue cannot be explained by its radicalism. Its real attraction for the millions who read it lies elsewhere—perhaps in its vivid recreation of "a slice of life" so horridly unfamiliar that it can be made to yield an exotic interest.) The sympathy of these ostensibly political writers with the revolutionary cause is often genuine, yet their understanding of its inner movement, intricate problems, and doctrinal and strategic motives is so deficient as to call into question their competence to deal with political material. In the complete works of the so-called "proletarian school" you will not find a single viable portrait of a Marxist intellectual or of any character in the revolutionary drama who, conscious of his historical role, is not a mere automaton of spontaneous class force or impulse.

What really happened in the nineteen-thirties is that due to certain events the public aspects of experience appeared more meaningful than its private aspects, and literature responded accordingly. But the subject of political art is *history*, which stands in the same relation to experience as fiction to biography; and just as surely as failure to generalize the biographical element thwarts the aspirant to fiction, so the ambition of the literary Left to create a political art was thwarted by its failure to lift experience to the level of history. (For the benefit of those people who habitually pause to insist on what they call "strictly literary values," I might add that by "history" in this connection I do not mean "history books" or anything resembling what is known as the "historical novel" or drama. A political art would succeed in lifting experience to the level of history if its perception of life—any life—were organized around a perspective relating the artist's sense of the *society* of the dead to his sense of the *society* of the living and the as yet unborn.)

Experience, in the sense of "felt life" rather than as life's total practice, is the main but by no means the total substance of literature. The part experience plays in the aesthetic sphere might well be compared to the part that the materialist conception of history assigns to economy. Experience, in the sense of this analogy, is the substructure of literature above which there rises a superstructure of values, ideas, and judgments—in a word, of the multiple forms of consciousness. But this base and summit are not stationary: they continually act and react upon each other.

It is precisely this superstructural level which is seldom reached by the typical American writer of the modern era. Most of the well-known reputations will bear out my point. Whether you approach a poet like Ezra Pound or novelists like Steinbeck and Faulkner, what is at once noticeable is the uneven, and at time quite distorted, development of the various elements that constitute literary talent. What is so exasperating about Pound's poetry, for example, is its peculiar combination of a finished technique (his special share in the distribution of experience) with amateurish and irresponsible ideas. It could be maintained that for sheer creative power Faulkner is hardly excelled by any living novelist, yet the diversity and wonderful intensity of the experience represented in his narratives cannot entirely make up for their lack of order, of a self-illuminating structure, and obscurity of value and meaning. One might naturally counter this criticism by stating that though Faulkner rarely or never sets forth values directly, they none the less exist in his work by implication. Yes, but implications incoherently expressed are no better than mystifications, and nowadays it is values that we can least afford to take on faith. Moreover, in a more striking manner perhaps than any of his contemporaries, Faulkner illustrates the tendency of the experiential mode, if pursued to its utmost extreme, to turn into its opposite through unconscious self-parody. In Faulkner the excess, the systematic inflation of the horrible is such a parody of experience. In Thomas Wolfe the same effect is produced by his swollen rhetoric and compulsion to repeat himself—and repetition is an obvious form of parody. This repetition-compulsion has plagued a good many American writers. Its first and most conspicuous victim, of course, was Whitman, who occasionally slipped into unintentional parodies of himself.

Yet there is a positive side to the primacy of experience in late American literature. For this primacy has conferred certain benefits upon it, of which none is more bracing than its relative immunity from abstraction and otherworldliness. The stream of life, unimpeded by the rocks and sands of ideology, flows through it freely. If inept in coping with the general, it particularizes not at all badly; and the assumptions of sanctity that so many European artists seem to require as a kind of guaranty of their professional standing are not readily conceded in the lighter and clearer American atmosphere. "Whatever may have been the case in years gone by," Whitman wrote in 1888, "the true use for the imaginative faculty of modern times is to give ultimate vivification to facts, to science, and to common lives, endowing them with glows and glories and final illustriousness which belong to every real thing,

22

and to real things only." As this statement was intended as a prophecy, it is worth noting that while the radiant endowments that Whitman speaks of—the "glows and glories and final illustriousness"—have not been granted, the desired and predicted vivification of facts, science, and common lives has in a measure been realized, though in the process Whitman's democratic faith has as often been belied as confirmed.

It is not the mere recoil from the inhibitions of puritan and neopuritan times that instigated the American search for experience. Behind it is the extreme individualism of a country without a long past to brood on, whose bourgeois spirit had not worn itself out and been debased in a severe struggle against an old culture so tenacious as to retain the power on occasion to fascinate and render impotent even its predestined enemies. Moreover, in contrast to the derangements that have continually shaken Europe, life in the United States has been relatively fortunate and prosperous. It is possible to speak of American history as "successful" history. Within the limits of the capitalist order—and until the present period the objective basis for a different social order simply did not exist here— the American people have been able to find definitive solutions for the great historical problems that faced them. Thus both the Revolutionary and the Civil War were complete actions that virtually abolished the antagonisms which had initially caused the breakdown of national equilibrium. In Europe similar actions have usually led to festering compromises that in the end reproduced the same conflicts in other forms.

It is plain that until very recently there has really been no urgent need in America for high intellectual productivity. Indeed, the American intelligentsia developed very slowly as a semi-independent grouping; and what is equally important, for more than a century now and especially since 1865, it has been kept at a distance from the machinery of social and political power. What this means is that insofar as it has been deprived of certain opportunities, it has also been sheltered and pampered. There was no occasion or necessity for the intervention of the intellectuals—it was not mentality that society needed most in order to keep its affairs in order. On the whole the intellectuals were left free to cultivate private interests, and, once the moral and aesthetic ban on certain types of exertion had been removed, uninterrruptedly to solicit individual experience. It is this lack of a sense of extremity and many-sided involvement which explains the peculiar shallowness of a good deal of American literary expression. If some conditions of insecurity have been known to retard and disarm the mind, so have some conditions of security. The question is not whether Americans have suffered less than Europeans, but of the quality of whatever suffering and happiness have fallen to their lot.

The consequence of all this has been that American literature has tended to make too much of private life, to impose on it, to scour it for meanings that it cannot always legitimately yield. Henry James was the first to make a cause, if not a fetish, of personal relations; and the justice of his case, despite his vaunted divergence from the pioneer type, is that of a pioneer too, for while Americans generally were still engaged in "gathering in the preparations and necessities" he resolved to seek out "the amenities and consummations." Furthermore, by exploiting in a fashion altogether his own the contingencies of private life that fell within his scope, he was able to dramatize the relation of the new world to the old, thus driving the wedge of historical consciousness into the very heart of the theme of experience. Later not a few attempts were made to combine experience with consciousness, to achieve the balance of thought and being characteristic of the great traditions of European art. But except for certain narratives of James and Melville, I know of very little American fiction which can unqualifiedly be said to have attained this end.

Since the decline of the regime of gentility many admirable works have been produced, but in the main it is the quantity of felt life comprised in them that satisfies, not their quality of belief or interpretive range. In poetry there is evidence of more distinct gains, perhaps because the medium has reached that late stage in its evolution when its chance of survival depends on its capacity to absorb ideas. The modern poetic styles—metaphysical and symbolist—depend on a conjunction of feeling and idea. But, generally speaking, bare experience is still the *Leitmotif* of the American writer, though the literary depression of recent years tends to show that this theme is virtually exhausted. At bottom it was the theme of the individual transplanted from an old culture taking inventory of himself and of his new surroundings. This inventory, this initial recognition and experiencing of oneself and one's surroundings, is all but complete now, and those who persist in going on with it are doing so out of mere routine and inertia.

The creative power of the cult of experience is almost spent, but what lies beyond it is still unclear. One thing, however, is certain: whereas in the past, throughout the nineteenth and well into the twentieth century, the nature of American literary life was largely determined by national forces, now it is international forces that have begun to exert a dominant influence. And in the long run it is in the terms of this historic change that the future course of American writing will define itself.

THE DARK LADY OF SALEM

> *Because I seek an image not a book . . .*
> —W. B. Yeats

Hawthorne is generally spoken of as a novelist of sin, but the truth is that he is not a novelist, at least not in the sense in which the term is commonly used, nor is sin wholly and unequivocally his subject. What that subject is remains to be defined, though by way of introduction it might be said that it is less a subject than a predicament. Or, better still, the predicament is the subject.

What is the intention of the novel as we have come to know it? In the broadest sense, it is to portray life as it is actually lived. Free access to experience is the necessary condition of the novel's growth as well as the objective guaranty of its significance; experience is at once its myth and its reason; and he who shuns experience is no more capable of a convincing performance in its sphere than a man unnerved by the sight of blood is capable of heroic feats on the battlefield. Now Hawthorne lived in an age when it was precisely experience—or, at any rate, those of its elements most likely to engage the interests of an artist—that was least at the disposal of the imaginative American, whose psychic resistance to its appeal was everywhere reinforced by the newness and bareness of the

27

national scene, by its much-lamented "paucity of ingredients." It is this privation that accounts for Hawthorne's chill ideality, for his tendency to cherish the fanciful at the expense of the substantial and to reduce the material world to the all-too-familiar abstractions of spiritual law and the moral conscience. Two strains mingle in his literary nature: the spectral strain of the Gothic tale and the pietistic strain of Christian allegory, and both contribute to his alienation from the real.*

Yet there is in this writer a submerged intensity and passion—a tangled imagery of unrest and longing for experience and regret at its loss which is largely ignored by those of his critics who place him too securely within the family-circle of the New England moralists. His vision of evil carries something more than a simple, one-way assertion of traditional principles; it carries their negation as well. He was haunted not only by the guilt of his desires but also by the guilt of his denial of them. The puritan in him grappled with the man of the nineteenth century—historically a man of appetite and perspective; and the former did not so easily pacify and curb the latter as is generally assumed.

The whole tone and meaning of Hawthorne's work, it seems to me, turns on this conflict.

In his own estimate he was a "romancer," and his insistence on designating himself as such should not be overlooked. Time and again he admonished his readers not to expect from him that "fidelity, not merely to the possible,

---

* In his *American Prose Masters,* W. C. Brownell observes that Hawthorne's particular genius took him out of the novelist's field altogether. "His novels are not novels. They have not the reality of novels, and they elude it not only in their personages but in their picture of life in general." But the fact is that Hawthorne's particular genius cannot be assessed apart from the forces that shaped its expression. If we accept Brownell's definition of the novel as the medium of the actual, it can be stated flatly that neither Hawthorne nor any of his contemporaries succeeded in mastering it.

but to the probable and ordinary course of man's existence" which is the mark of the novelist. He took pains to distinguish between the romance and the novel in order to lay claim, though not without due apologies, to the latitude inherent in the earlier genre. Yet he was fully aware of its deficiencies, aware that the freedom it afforded was more apparent than real, committing him to all sorts of dodges and retreats to which his artist's conscience could not be reconciled. This explains his habit of referring to his own compositions in a disparaging manner as "fancy-pictures" that could not survive a close comparison with the actual events of real lives.

Even while writing *The Scarlet Letter,* the theme of which suited him perfectly, he publicly regretted the "folly" of flinging himself back into a distant age and attempting to create "a semblance of a world out of airy matter." He would have been far better served, he goes on to confess in that superb essay, *The Custom House,* had he sought his themes in the "warm materiality" of the daily scene. "The fault," he concludes, "was mine. The page of life that was spread out before me seemed dull and commonplace, only because I had not fathomed its deeper import. A better book than I shall ever write was there. . . . At some future day, it may be, I shall remember a few scattered fragments and broken paragraphs, and write them down, and find the letters turn to gold upon the page." But he was fated to be disappointed. The golden flow of reality never suffused his pages. Instead of entering the waking world of the novel, he remained to the last a "romancer" under the spell of that shadowy stuff which he at once loved and hated.

In the development of narrative-prose his place is decidedly among the pre-novelists—a position which he holds not alone but in the company of Poe and Melville and virtually the entire clan of classic American writers who, at one time or another, turned their hand to the making of fiction. The fact is that no novels, properly speaking, were produced in America until late in the nineteenth century, when the moralistic, semiclerical outlook which had so long dominated the native culture-heroes finally began to give way. The freedom promised by the Transcendentalist movement of the mid-century had not gone beyond a certain philosophical warmth and ardor of purpose. Though this movement expanded American thought, in itself this did not suffice to release the novelistic function. The release was effected only after the Civil War, when the many-sided expansion of American life created a new set of circumstances more favorable to artists whose business is with the concrete manifestations of the real and with its everyday textures. Then it was that James and Howells, susceptible, in different degrees, to the examples of European writing, came forward with new ideas, plans, and recipes.

Hawthorne's isolation from experience incapacitated him as a novelist. Yet he longed to break through this isolation, searching for the key that would let him out of the dungeon and enable him to "open intercourse with the world." "I have not lived," he cried, "but only dreamed of living. . . . I have seen so little of the world that I have nothing but thin air to concoct my stories of. . . ." Even the moderately candid biographies of him show that such protests were typical of his state of mind. And since these protests also inform his fiction, even if only in a tortuous and contradictory fashion, it can be said that his basic concern as a writer, though expressed in the traditional-moral terms of the problem of sin, was at bottom with the problem of experience—experience, however, not in the sense of its open representation in the manner of a novelist, but simply in the sense of debating its pros and cons, of examining good and evil, its promise and threat.

This preparatory scrutiny of experience constitutes his real subject, which is obscured by his creative means of allegoric construction and lavish employment of fantasy. His subject and the method he adopted to give it fictional form are incongruously related, but it was the only method available to him in his situation and, despite its faults, it permitted the growth of a novelistic embryo in each of his romances. That which is most actual in his work is comprised in these embryos; the rest—coming under the head of "romance"—is composed by his Gothic machinery and fed by the ceaseless pullulations of the sin-dogma. Knowingly or not, he indicated his own practice in remarking: "Realities keep in the rear, and put forward an advance-guard of show and humbug."

But the split in his emotional and intellectual nature prevented him from ever resolving the conflict of value and impulse implicit in his subject. All he could do was reproduce his predicament within his creations. On the one hand he thought it desirable "to live throughout the whole range of one's faculties and sensibilities" and, on the other, to play the part of a spiritualized Paul Pry "hovering invisible around men and women, witnessing their deeds, searching into their hearts, borrowing brightness from their felicity and shade from their sorrow, *and retaining no emotion peculiar to himself.*" In other words, he wanted the impossible—to enjoy the warmth and vitality of experience without exposing himself to its perils. His entire heritage predisposed him to regard a welcoming and self-offering attitude to experience as the equivalent of a state of sin; and though he was inclined to doubt the justice and validity of this cruelly schematic equation, its sway over him nevertheless told in the end. It barred him from any patent commitment to that program of personal liberation which his successors in the American creative line were later to adopt and elaborate into peculiarly indigenous forms of literary art. Is experience identical with sin?—and if so, is sin the doom of man or his salvation? To these queries he provided no clear rejoinder, but his bent was to say one thing on the surface of his work, on the level of its manifest content, while saying something else in its depths, in its latent meanings. He tried to serve at once the old and the new gods, and in the main it is within the active play of this ambivalence,

31

of this sundered devotion, that he achieved his unique color and interest. His incubus he taught to poetize.

The constraint under which he labored had its source, of course, in the old Calvinist faith, but he was born too late to know it for what it once was. Of religion, indeed, he knew little beyond its fears. Originally a powerful vision of man's relation to God, the puritan orthodoxy was now reduced to a narrow moral scheme with clerical trappings. And Hawthorne's dilemma was that though the supernatural hardly existed for him in any realm save that of the fanciful, he was none the less unable to free himself from the perception of human destiny in terms of sin and redemption, sacrilege and consecration. The sacramental wine had turned to poison in his cup. His dreams abounded in images of his ancestors rising from their graves and of himself walking down Main Street in a shroud. No wonder, then, that he tended to conceive of the past as a menace to the living, as a force the ghastly fascination of which must be resisted.

The House of the Seven Gables is one long symbolization of this feeling. "In this age," preaches Holgrave, the young man who stands for the renovation of life, "the moss-grown and rotten Past is to be torn down, and lifeless institutions to be thrust out of the way, and their dead corpses buried, and everything to begin anew. . . . What slaves we are to bygone times—to Death. . . . We live in dead men's houses . . . as in this of the Seven Gables. . . . The house ought to be purified with fire,—purified till only its ashes remain." Still, at the same time as Hawthorne abused the past and remonstrated against its morbid influences, he continued to indulge his taste for gloom and moldiness—for "old ideals and loitering paces and muffled tones." And as the years passed he yielded more and more to this tendency, with the result that in his last phase his mind faltered—it had lost, as he himself admitted, its fine edge and temper—and he could produce nothing but such fragmentary and essentially

32

pointless allegories as *Septimius Felton* and *The Dolliver Romance*.

The conflict in him is clearly between a newborn secular imagination, as yet untried and therefore permeated with the feeling of shock and guilt, and the moribund religious tradition of old New England. It is a conflict which has seldom been detected by his critics, who have for the most part confounded his inner theme of experience with the all-too-apparent theme of sin. Yet the two themes, regardless of their mutual relation from a theological standpoint, are quite distinct as life-elements—though Hawthorne could not but confuse them. Perhaps it is this that was intuitively sensed by D. H. Lawrence, when he spoke of the duplicity of that "blue-eyed *Wunderkind* of a Nathaniel," thus construing as double-dealing a double-mindedness the roots of which lie deep in American history. But the melodramatic twist of Lawrence's insights is scarcely a valid reason for discounting them. He accurately noted the split in Hawthorne between his outward conformity and the "impeccable truth of his art-speech," between his repressed under-meanings and the moonshiny spirituality of his surface.

The evidence, of course, is in the tales and romances. There is one heroine they bring to life who is possibly the most resplendent and erotically forceful woman in American fiction. She dominates all the other characters because she alone personifies the contrary values that her author attached to experience. Drawn on a scale larger than reality, she is essentially a mythic being, the incarnation of hidden longings and desires, as beautiful, we are repeatedly told, as she is "inexpressibly terrible," a temptress offering the ascetic sons of the puritans the "treasure-trove of a great sin."

We come to know this dark lady under four different names—as Beatrice in the story *Rappaccini's Daughter*, Hester in *The Scarlet Letter*, Zenobia in *The Blithedale*

33

Romance, and Miriam in *The Marble Faun.* Her unity as a character is established by the fact that in each of her four appearances she exhibits the same physical and mental qualities and plays substantially the same role. Hawthorne's description of her is wonderfully expressive in the fullness of its sensual imaginings. He is ingenious in devising occasions for celebrating her beauty, and conversely, for denigrating, albeit in equivocal language, her blonde rival—the dove-like, virginal, snow-white maiden of New England. But the two women stand to each other in the relation of the damned to the saved, so that inevitably the dark lady comes to a bad end while the blonde is awarded all the prizes—husband, love, and absolute exemption from moral guilt. There is obviously an obsessive interest here in the psychosexual polarity of dark and fair with its symbolism of good and evil—a polarity which in Fenimore Cooper's treatment (in *The Last of the Mohicans* and *The Deerslayer*) is little more than a romantic convention but which both in Hawthorne and in Melville (Hautia and Yillah in *Mardi* and Isabel and Lucy in *Pierre*) acquires a newly intensive meaning.

Beatrice, of *Rappaccini's Daughter,* is as luxuriant as any of the gem-like flowers in her father's garden of poisonous plants. She looks "redundant with life, health, and energy . . . beautiful as the day, with a bloom so deep and vivid that one shade more would have been too much"; her voice, "rich as a tropical sunset," makes her lover Giovanni "think of deep hues of purple or crimson and of perfumes heavily delectable." Hester, of *The Scarlet Letter,* is "tall, with a figure of perfect elegance on a large scale. She had dark and abundant hair, so glossy that it threw off the sunshine with a gleam, and a face which besides being beautiful from regularity of feature and richness of complexion, had the impressiveness belonging to a marked brow. . . . She had in her nature a rich, voluptuous, Oriental characteristic." In the redundancy of her charms Zenobia, of *The Blithedale Romance,* is fully the equal of Hester Prynne. "Zenobia was an admirable . . . a magnificent figure of a woman, just on the hither verge of her maturity . . . her hand, though very soft, was larger than most women would like to have . . . though not a whit too large in proportion with the spacious plan of her development . . . the native glow of coloring in her cheeks, and even the flesh-warmth of her round arms, and what was visible of her full bust—in a word, her womanliness incarnate—compelled me sometimes to close my eyes. . . . One felt an influence breathing out of her such as we might suppose to come from Eve, when she was just made . . . a certain warm and rich characteristic . . . the whole woman was alive with a passionate intensity in which her beauty culminated. Any passion would have become her well; and passionate love, perhaps, best of all." And Miriam, of *The Marble Faun*, also had "a great deal of color in her nature . . . a beautiful woman . . . with dark eyes . . . black, abundant hair . . . a dark glory."

It is plain that the physical characteristics of these four heroines are interchangeable, and this cannot be due to poverty of invention on Hawthorne's part. What it suggests, rather, is a strong fixation on a certain type of woman, in every way the opposite of the sexually anesthetic females to whom he officially paid homage.* The

---

* In this connection a revealing passage from W. D. Howells' *Literary Friends and Acquaintance* is worth citing. Howells is telling of his first meeting with Hawthorne in 1860: "With the abrupt transition of his talk throughout, he [Hawthorne] began to speak of women, and said he had never seen a woman whom he thought quite beautiful. In the same way he spoke of the New England temperament, and suggested that the apparent coldness in it was also real, and that the suppression of emotion for generations would extinguish it at last." Psychologically speaking, the second remark might be taken as a sufficient explanation of the first. On the other hand, perhaps Hawthorne meant to say that no woman he had ever met in the flesh was quite as resplendent as his imagined dark lady.

35

dark lady is above all an ambivalent love-object*; but beyond that she makes visible that desire for an open-
handed conduct of life and individual fulfillment which
was in later years to become the major concern of American writing. Reduced to more realistic proportions but
none the less still invested with mythic powers, she reappears, in such novels as Sherwood Anderson's *Dark Laughter* and *Many Marriages,* in the part of the ideal love-
partner for whom thwarted husbands desert their wives;
and a character like Hemingway's Maria (*For Whom the
Bell Tolls*)—likewise not a "real" person but a dream-
image of sexual bliss—is clearly in her line of descent. In
her latter-day mutations, however, the sinister side of this
heroine has been obliterated. She is now wholly affirmed.

But insofar as they no longer threaten us, these idealized modern women have also ceased to be thoughtful.
The Anderson and Hemingway girls leave us without
any distinct impression of their minds, whereas the dark
lady of Salem displays mental powers that are the counterpart of her physical vitality. Invariably she dominates,
or seeks to dominate, the men she loves, and her intellectual range equals and at times even exceeds theirs. She
not only acts but thinks passionately, solving the problem
of the relation between the sexes in a radical fashion and
subverting established values and standards. After being
cast out by the community, Hester, we are told, "assumed

---

* Her type is not unknown of course in Victorian fiction, from
Trollope to Hardy. She also enters the folklore of the Anglo-
Saxon countries as the villainous "dark vampire" of the early
American films and popular romances. It is interesting to note
that in the 1920's the glamorous (the "hot") blonde replaces
the mysterious and voluptuous brunette as the carrier of the
sexually potent and dangerous. In Anita Loos' *Gentlemen
Prefer Blondes* the usurpation has already gone so far that it is
taken for granted. This reversal of roles may well be due to
the newly won sexual freedom of the post-war era, a freedom
which brought the sexual element to the light of day and thus
ended its hitherto exclusive identification with the secrets of
the night.

a freedom of speculation . . . which our forefathers, had they known it, would have held to be a deadlier crime than that stigmatized by the scarlet letter"; Zenobia, who is something of a litterateur and a crusader for women's rights,* has an aptitude for extreme ideas that fill her interlocutors with dismay; and Miriam evolves a conception of sin which amounts to a justification, for she takes the view that sin is a means of educating and improving the personality.

The dark lady is a rebel and an emancipator; but precisely for this reason Hawthorne feels the compulsion to destroy her. *He thus converts the principle of life, of experience, into a principle of death.* Incessantly haunted by the wrongs of the past, by the memory of such brutal deeds directly implicating the founders of his family as the witchcraft-trials and the oppression of the Quakers, this repentant puritan is nevertheless impelled by an irresistible inner need to reproduce the very same ancestral pattern in his work. Roused by long-forgotten fears and superstitions, he again traces the footprints of the devil and hears demonic laughter in the woods as darkness falls. His story of the dark lady renews, in all essentials, the persecution of the Salem witches. Beatrice is "as lovely as the dawn and gorgeous as the sunset," yet the "rich perfume of her breath blasts the very air" and to embrace her is to die. Passionate love becomes Zenobia best, yet through insinuating symbols she is pictured as a sorceress. She wears an exotic flower in her hair, and perhaps if this talismanic flower were snatched away she would "vanish or be transformed into something else." Miriam, too, has the "faculty of bewitching people." When her nerves give way and she fancies herself unseen, she seeks relief

---

* This is the basis of the widespread impression that she is modelled after Margaret Fuller. Henry James thought there was no truth in the legend. Hawthorne's references to the Boston sibyl in his notebooks are uniformly unkind; he describes her as devoid of the "charm of womanhood" and as a "great humbug" to boot.

in "fits of madness horrible to behold." Such is the twice-told tale of the dark lady. The victim, in her earlier incarnations, of grim black-browed puritan magistrates, she is now searched out by a secluded New England author who condemns her because she coerces his imagination.

Her figure is first evoked by Hawthorne in *Rappaccini's Daughter* (1844), an entirely fantastic tale generally ranked among the most brilliantly effective of his earlier writings. Beatrice is the daughter of a malignant old professor, who, in his search of fearsome secrets, is experimenting with the medicinal properties of poisonous plants. On coming to Padua, the student Giovanni rents a room the window of which overlooks Rappaccini's garden. Though unaware of the real nature of the flowers in this garden, he is at once troubled by their strange and rampant bloom.—"The aspect of one and all of them dissatisfied him; their gorgeousness seemed fierce, passionate, and even unnatural. There was hardly an individual shrub which a wanderer, straying by himself through a forest, would not have been startled to find growing wild, as if an unearthly face had glared at him out of the thicket." His initial impression of Beatrice is that she is but another flower—"the human sister of these vegetable ones, as beautiful as they, more beautiful than the richest of them, but still to be touched only with a glove, nor to be approached without a mask"; and when night closes in, he dreams of a rich flower and a lovely girl. "Flower and maiden were different and yet the same, and fraught with some peculiar peril in either shape." In time, as Giovanni ventures into the garden, he learns that the flowers are deadly. But he is now in love with Beatrice and tormented by the suspicion that she possesses the same fatal attributes. Can such dreadful peculiarities in her physical nature exist, he asks himself, without some corresponding "monstrosity of soul"? The day comes when after many tests he is at last sure that not only is she poisonous but that she had begun to instill her poison into his system. He

38

procures an antidote which he forces her to drink. But it is too late to save her, for "so radically had her earthly part been wrought upon by Rappaccini's skill, that as poison had been her life, so the powerful antidote was death; and thus the poor victim of man's ingenuity and of thwarted nature . . . perished there, at the feet of her father and Giovanni."

No summary can give an adequate sense of the exotic light in which this story is drenched, nor of the extravagantly erotic associations of its imagery. It opens with the "peephole" motif, so typical of Hawthorne. ("Sometimes through a peephole I have caught a glimpse of the real world . . ." he wrote to Longfellow.) At first it is only from the outside—through a window—that Giovanni dares to peer into this "Eden of poisonous flowers," which Freudians would have no trouble at all translating into a garden of genitalia. But whether interpreted in a Freudian manner or not, its mystery is easily unraveled. What is this Eden if not the garden of experience, of the knowledge of good and evil. Giovanni is tempted to enter it, only to discover that its gorgeous flowers are emblems of sin and that the gorgeous Beatrice embodies all that is forbidden. She has succeeded in enticing him into a "region of unspeakable horror," but it is she who is doomed, while he, being innocent, escapes. The wages of sin is death.

To be sure, there are other readings of this story. The traditional one simply takes at face value Hawthorne's stated intention, his "message" warning against such unscrupulous love of power and knowledge as is manifested in Rappaccini. The old professor, who is a shadow character, is thus put in the foreground, while Beatrice, who is the real protagonist, is reduced to the role of a mere passive victim of her father's monomaniacal ambition. Needless to say, this approach ignores the story's specific content for the sake of its abstract and, it should be remarked, utterly commonplace moral. It fails to account for the mystic sensuality, the hallucinated atmos-

39

phere, and the intertwining symbolism of flower and maiden. No, this business of the wizard Rappaccini and his poisons is just so much flummery and Gothic sleight-of-hand. Its use is that of an "alibi" for the author, who transforms Beatrice into a monster in order to punish her for tempting Giovanni. Actually it is her beauty that Hawthorne cannot forgive her.

The flower-symbolism of this tale is repeated in the later romances of the dark lady. So resplendent is the scarlet token of shame worn by Hester Prynne that it might well be a flower in Rappaccini's garden formed to spell the letter A. ("On the breast of her gown, in fine red cloth, surrounded with an elaborate embroidery and fantastic flourishes of gold thread, there appeared the letter A. It was so artistically done, and with so much fertility and gorgeous luxuriance of fancy. . . .") And, again, much is made in *The Blithedale Romance* of the single flower that adorns Zenobia's hair.—"It was a hot-house flower, an outlandish flower, a flower of the tropics, such as appeared to have sprung passionately from a soil the very weeds of which would be fervid and spicy . . . so brilliant, so rare, so costly. . . ." It is manifestly a flower of a preternatural order, a kind of *mana*-object, an instrument of magic and witches' work.

As compared to the subsequent full-length versions of the same theme, the story of Beatrice is but a primitive fantasy. There is a gap between *Rappaccini's Daughter* and *The Scarlet Letter,* which was written six years later and which is the most truly novelistic of Hawthorne's romances. Its concrete historical setting gives it greater density of material and sharpness of outline; and largely because of this gain in reality, Hester Prynne is the least symbolically overladen and distorted of the four heroines who share in the character of the dark lady. There is nothing satanic about her motives and she is the only one who, far from being ultimately spurned, is justified instead.

There are ambiguities in *The Scarlet Letter,* as in all

of Hawthorne, yet it is possible to say that it represents his furthest advance in affirming the rights of the individual. Known as a story of the expiation of a sin, it is quite as much an analysis of this sin as a "kind of typical illusion." It is the Reverend Mr. Dimmesdale, his brain reeling from ghostly visions, who in his repentance plies a bloody scourge on his own shoulders; Hester, on the other hand, is ready to reject the puritan morality altogether, to make a clean sweep of the past and to escape from the settlement in order to fulfill her love without shame or fear. Her pariah-status in the community is not productive of remorse and humility. On the contrary, we are told that "standing alone in the world . . . the world's law was no law for her mind. . . . In her lonesome cottage, by the seashore, thoughts visited her, such as dared enter no other dwelling in New England."

This is best shown in Chapters XVII and XVIII of the novel when Hester finally persuades the minister that the only way he could rid himself of Chillingsworth's persecution is to desert his congregation and return to England. At first he thinks that she bids him go alone, whereupon he protests that he has not the strength or courage to embark on such a venture. At this point she reveals her plan, proving that she does not recognize her guilt, that for her nothing has changed, that in fact "the whole seven years of outlawry and ignominy had been little other than a preparation for this very hour."—But some of the passages that follow are worth quoting at length.

> He repeated the word.
> "Alone, Hester!"
> "Thou shalt not go alone!" answered she, in a deep whisper. Then all was spoken!
> Arthur Dimmesdale gazed into Hester's face with a look in which hope and joy shone out, indeed, but with fear between them, and a kind of horror at her boldness, who had spoken what he vaguely hinted at but dared not speak.
> But Hester Prynne, with a mind of native courage and activity, and for so long a period not merely estranged, but outlawed from society, had habituated herself to such latitude of

speculation as was altogether foreign to the clergyman. . . . For years past she had looked from this estranged point of view at human institutions, and whatever priests or legislators had established. . . . The tendency of her fate has been to set her free.

"Thou wilt go," said Hester, calmly, as he met her glance.

The decision once made, a glow of strange enjoyment threw its flickering brightness over the trouble of his breast. It was the exhilarating effect—upon a prisoner just escaped from the dungeon of his own heart—of breathing the wild, free atmosphere of an unredeemed, unchristianized, lawless region. . . .

"Do I feel joy again?" cried he, wondering at himself. "Methinks the germ of it was dead in me! O, Hester, thou art my better angel! I seem to have flung myself—sick, sinstained, and sorrow-blackened—down upon these forest-leaves, and to have risen up all made anew, and with new powers to glorify Him that hath been merciful! This is already the better life. Why did we not find it sooner?"

"Let us not look back," answered Hester Prynne. "The past is gone! . . . See! With this symbol I undo it all, and make it as it had never been!"

So speaking, she undid the clasp that fastened the scarlet letter, and taking it from her bosom, threw it to a distance among the withered leaves. . . . The stigma gone, Hester heaved a deep, long sigh, in which the burden of shame and anguish departed from her spirit. O exquisite relief! . . . By another impulse she took off the formal cap that confined her hair; and down it fell upon her shoulders, dark and rich. . . . There played around her mouth and beamed out of her eyes, a radiant and tender smile, that seemed gushing from the very heart of womanhood. A crimson flush was glowing on her cheeks, that had been long so pale. Her sex, her youth, and the whole richness of her beauty, came back from what men call the irrevocable past, and clustered themselves, with her maiden hope and a happiness before unknown, within the magic circle of this hour.

This unregenerate temptress knows her power, but in the end Dimmesdale cheats her of her triumph by publicly confessing his sin on the scaffold; and that, of course, is *his* triumph. This thin-skinned clergyman is the ancestor of all those characters in Henry James who invent excruciatingly subtle reasons for renouncing their heart's desire once they are on the verge of attaining it. But in James there are also other characters who, while preserving Dimmesdale's complex qualities of conscience and sensibility, finally do succeed in overcoming this tendency to renunciation. Lambert Strether of *The Ambassadors* and Milly Theale of *The Wings of the Dove,* whose ideal aim is "to achieve a sense of having lived," are plainly cases of reaction against Hawthorne's plaint: "I have not lived but only dreamed of living!"

This link with James is further evidence that, though in no position to show his hand and not even fully conscious of what was at stake, Hawthorne dealt with the problem of sin mainly insofar as it served him as a mold for the problem of experience. It is difficult to believe in the sins committed by his characters for the simple reason that he hardly believes in them himself. Consider how he stacks the cards, how he continually brings up extenuating circumstances and even lapses into telltale defensive statements, so that before long we cannot but lose the conviction of evil and corruption. Who, actually, are his sinners? The minor figures cannot, of course, be taken into account in this respect, for, like Chillingsworth, Westervelt, Miriam's model and even Judge Pyncheon, they are nothing more than conventional villains, and at that most of them are so unreal that their conduct is of little consequence. It is only the protagonists, then, who count. But of these, with the exception of Dimmesdale, there is scarcely one who can be objectively regarded as a wrongdoer. Among the women only Hester's guilt is definitely established, yet even she is shown to have so many rights on her side that it is impossible to see in her anything more portentous than a violator of the communal *mores*. It is not, however, by their flouting of the communal *mores* that we judge the great transgressors pictured in literature. These big biters into the apple inevitably sin against the Holy Ghost.

Zenobia and Miriam wholly exemplify Hawthorne's bias against the dark lady, a bias which, instead of being supported and objectified by a credible presentation of her

43

misdeeds, is limited in its expression to atmospheric effects, insinuations, and rumors. He wants to destroy the dark lady at the same time that he wants to glorify her; hence his indictment of her is never really driven home. This divided intention cannot but impair the dramatic structures of *The Blithedale Romance* and *The Marble Faun,* and these two narratives are in fact much inferior to *The Scarlet Letter.*

But the *Romance,* with its marvelous sense of place and weather and with its contrasted tableaux of town and country, has a unique appeal of its own. Both James and Lawrence have testified to its attraction. The former speaks of it as "leaving in the memory an impression analogous to that of an April day—an alternation of brightness and shadow, of broken sun-patches and sprinkling clouds." James also thought that in Zenobia Hawthorne made his nearest approach to the complete creation of a character. But this vivid brunette is treated with much less sympathy than Hester—and perhaps the reason is that since she exerts greater sexual power she must needs be subjected to firmer measures of control. At any rate, his attitude toward her is markedly more subjective, and this note of subjectivity is one of the charms of the *Romance,* the unfailing charm of the confessional tone and of the personal modulation. The story is told through a narrator by the name of Miles Coverdale, a minor Boston poet in whom one easily discerns many features of the author.

No sooner does Coverdale come upon Zenobia in Blithedale—a Utopian colony inhabited by a "little army of saints and martyrs"—than her beauty moves him to rhapsodic appreciation; he is in a fever of susceptibility, and the very next day a fit of sickness lays him low. His illness and exhaustion render him even more sensitive—morbidly so—to what he calls "Zenobia's sphere." (What a master stroke, this episode of Coverdale's illness, with its suggestions of a rite of passage from one mode of life to another!) Obviously infatuated with her, he is not the man to submit to such a feeling. By

44

what is plainly a psychological detour—analysts would see in it an example of protective displacement—he persuades himself that his real attachment is to Zenobia's half-sister, the mediumistic, shadowy snow-maiden who is the Prissy of the tale. This convenient self-deception permits him to covet Zenobia and to pry into her affairs without in any way committing himself to her—for how could he, a paleface poet with overcharged scruples, make up to a woman who is "passionate, luxurious, lacking simplicity, not deeply refined, incapable of pure and perfect taste"? Moreover, as if to spare him further trouble, both females fall in love not with him but with the fanatical reformer Hollingsworth, who is a mere stick of a character, a travesty as a reformer and even worse travesty as a lover. The emotional economy of this story is throughout one of displacement. It is evident on every page that the only genuine relationship is that of Coverdale to Zenobia; the rest is mystification. But the whole point of Coverdale's behavior is to avoid involvement. As Zenobia tells him in one of the final bang-up scenes, his real game is "to grope for human emotions in the dark corners of the heart"—strictly in the hearts of other people, to be sure. He plays perfectly the role of the ideal Paul Pry that Hawthorne envisaged for himself in the earlier passages of his journals.

Though vowing that he adores the ethereal Priscilla, Coverdale is nevertheless quite adept at belittling her by means of invidious comparisons that strike home despite their seemingly general reference. Some finicky people, he reflects after his first encounter with Zenobia, might consider her wanting in softness and delicacy, but the truth is that "we find enough of these attributes everywhere; preferable . . . was Zenobia's bloom, health, and vigor, which she possessed in such overflow that a man might well have fallen in love with her for their sake only." And again: "We seldom meet with women nowadays, and in this country, who impress us as being women at all;—their sex fades away and goes for nothing . . . a

45

certain warm and rich characteristic seems to have been refined away out of the feminine system." Finally, in view of these frequent digs at Prissy, there can be no doubt that Westervelt, the villain of the piece, is really speaking for Coverdale when he describes her as "one of those delicate, young creatures, not uncommon in New England, and whom I suppose to have become what we find them by the gradual refining away of the physical system among your women. Some philosophers choose to glorify this habit of body by terming it spiritual; but in my opinion, it is rather the effect of unwholesome food, bad air, lack of outdoor exercise, and neglect of bathing, on the part of these damsels and their female progenitors, all resulting in a kind of hereditary dyspepsia. Zenobia, with her uncomfortable surplus of vitality, is far the better model of womanhood."

But this "better model of womanhood" commits suicide for want of love, while the obstreperous Hollingsworth is collared by Prissy and dragged to the altar. The puritan morality of predestination takes its toll as the story closes. Humanity is divided into the damned and the saved, irretrievably so, and never the twain shall meet. Yet the *Romance,* despite its mechanically enforced moral lessons, stands out among Hawthorne's works for its outspokenness and for its bold and free characterization of Coverdale and Zenobia. In its painful doubleness, in its feeling of combined attraction and repulsion, the relationship between these two characters is one of the most meaningful and seminal in American literature. It is intrinsically the relationship between New England and the world, and again the connection with James comes to mind. Zenobia can be understood as an earlier and cruder version of Madame de Vionnet (of *The Ambassadors*), whose worldly motives and passionate nature Lambert Strether finally comes to understand and to accept; and Coverdale, too, is reproduced in James, and not in one type alone. One recognizes his kinship with Strether, who has overcome the obsession with sin and is priming himself to enter forbidden territory, no less than with such a curious figure as the spying, eavesdropping protagonist of *The Sacred Fount,* whose neurotic fear and envy of life find an outlet in a mania of snooping and prying into the lives of his neighbors. In this nameless Jamesian snooper the "peephole" motif reaches its culmination: it has become his medium of existence and his intellectual rationale besides.

In *The Marble Faun* Hawthorne resumes his story of the dark lady, and his attitude to her is now formulated in more logical terms. The conception of sin as an "instrument most effective in the education of intellect and soul" is openly expounded and affirmed by Miriam, whereas the snow-maiden Hilda, who is a purist and perfectionist, defends to the last the old puritan ethic. What Miriam advocates is the right of the personality to that self-knowledge and self-development which only the process of experience can provide. But she too, like Hester, is in the end sentenced by the author to life-long suffering and expiation of her sin. Unlike Hester's sin, however, Miriam's is utterly chimerical, fabricated out of whole cloth by the Gothic machinery of horror; what alone is real is her defiance of the ancestral taboos.

The part of the male evildoer in *The Marble Faun* is taken by Donatello, the innocent, faun-like, quasi-mythical Italian who is drawn by Miriam to commit a crime and is thus brought within the confines of "sinful, sorrowful mentality." It is the story, of course, of the fall of man, with the dark lady cast in the dual role of Eve and the serpent. Hilda and the sculptor Kenyon are the onlookers and commentators on the action. Presented as models of virtue, they are actually an insufferable pair of prigs, especially Hilda, who is in fact one of the grimmest figures in Hawthorne, despite all the proper talk about her dovelike nature. Symbolically enough, this militant virgin dwells in a tower which is continually referred to as the "young girl's eyerie," and from this high vantage-point she surveys the conduct of mankind with the self-assurance of a moral millionaire. The sculptor, to be sure, tends to sympathize with Miriam, but Hilda never fails to pull him up short. The whole issue is summed up perfectly in the following dialogue between them:

"Ah, Hilda," said Kenyon, "you do not know, for you could never learn it from your own heart, which is all purity and rectitude, what a mixture of good and evil there may be in things evil; and how the greatest criminal, if you look at his conduct from his own point of view, or from any side-point, may seem not so unquestionably guilty, after all. So with Miriam, so with Donatello. They are, perhaps, partners in what we must call awful guilt; and yet, I will own to you,— when I think of the original cause, the motives, the feelings, the sudden concurrence of circumstances thrusting them onward, the urgency of the moment, and the sublime unselfishness on either part,—I know not well how to distinguish it from much that the world calls heroism. Might we not render some such verdict as this?—'Worthy of Death, but not unworthy of Love!'"

"Never!" answered Hilda, looking at the matter through the clear crystal medium of her own integrity. "This thing, as regards its causes, is all a mystery to me, and must remain so. But there is, I believe, only one right and only one wrong; and I do not understand, and may God keep me from understanding, how two things so totally unlike can be mistaken for one another; nor how two mortal foes, such as Right and Wrong surely are, can work together in the same deed. . . ."

"Alas for human nature, then!" said Kenyon, sadly. . . . "I have always felt you, my dear friend, a terribly severe judge, and have been perplexed to conceive how such tender sympathy could coexist with the remorselessness of a steel blade. You need no mercy, and therefore know not how to show any."

"That sounds like a bitter gibe," said Hilda, with the tears springing to her eyes. "But I cannot help it. It does not alter my perception of the truth. If there be any such dreadful mixture as you affirm—and which appears to me almost more shocking than pure evil,—then the good is turned to poison, not the evil to wholesomeness."

It is against such pharisaical moralism as Hilda displays that Hawthorne reacted in creating the figure of the dark lady, yet he could never muster the resolution to repudiate Hilda openly. Hence the dark lady, too, is inevitably stricken down by the same minatory code. Miriam pleads that the crime joining her to Donatello was "a blessing in disguise" in that it brought "a simple and imperfect nature to a point of feeling and intelligence which it could have reached under no other discipline." But her pleas are of no avail—in the end she is destroyed. And how illusory is the crime of which she is accused, with its horror-romanticism of the murder of a timeless wizard who has in some inexplicable way gained an ascendancy over her. And this in what is presumably a serious novel of crime and punishment! One might claim, of course, that the failure of actuality at this crucial turn of the plot is nothing more than a defect in the story-teller's art, a carryover from the obsolescent Gothic technique. But it is precisely Hawthorne's persistent reliance on this technique which is so revealing of his real situation. It seems to me that he is unable to authenticate Miriam's guilt for the quite obvious reason that her beauty and love of life already sufficiently condemn her in his eyes. In other words, it is not her deeds but her very existence which is the supreme provocation and the supreme crime.

The critics of the school of "original sin" have for some years now tried to present Hawthorne as a kind of puritan Dostoevsky. But this comparison will not stand the test of analysis. In their eagerness to make ideological capital out of Hawthorne's "traditionalism," these critics overlook one vital distinction: whereas in Dostoevsky's case the awareness of sin flows from a mighty effort to regain a metaphysical and religious consciousness, in Hawthorne this awareness is at the point of dissolution. What is behind it is no genuine moral passion nor a revival of dogma but a fear of life induced by narrow circumstances and morbid memories of the past. The faith of his forefathers had lost its rational appeal, yet psychologically it still ruled and confined him. Hence the inherited beliefs appear in his work as spectres rather than as convictions.

A literature of sin is most naturally developed in a society suffering from a surfeit of experience—an excess which it cannot control because of a derangement of

49

values. This was the condition of Russian society in Dostoevsky's time; and it is this unlimited availability of experience, amounting almost to anarchy, which enabled the Russian novelist to materialize his themes of sin and evil. We believe in the sins of Stavrogin, Raskolnikov, and the Karamazovs because they are actualized within the experiential realm, the only realm in which significant actions can be truly confirmed. Now if regarded from this point of view, the American romancer must be placed at the opposite pole from the Russian novelist. The society to which he belonged suffered not from a surfeit but from poverty of experience; and, far from being too fluid, its values were altogether too rigid. His problem was simpler than Dostoevsky's as well as radicaly different in nature. It was not an exceptional but necessarily a typical problem—typical, despite all variations, of America's creative writers in the nineteenth century and in the early decades of the twentieth. It can be defined as the problem of the re-conquest, of the reacquisition of experience in its cultural, aesthetic, and, above all, subjective aspects. For this is the species of experience which had gradually been lost to the migrant European man in the process of subjugating and settling the new world.

Van Wyck Brooks has described Hawthorne as the "most deeply planted of American writers." But this is true only in the sense that he is the most deeply and vividly local. He rifled the hive of New England honey, but he was quite indifferent to the wider ranges of the national scene. His is the "sweet flavor," to use one of his own similes, of "a frost-bitten apple, such as one picks up under the tree in December." It is the chill yet mellow flavor of the Salem centuries. On this side of him he indeed sums up and closes the puritan cycle; but from another angle of vision he can be seen to be precursive of the later and more positive interests of American letters. Times past are mirrored in the dark lady's harsh fate, yet in her mystic sensuality she speaks of things to come.

50

THE HEIRESS OF ALL THE AGES

Henry James is not fully represented in his novels by any one single character, but of his principal heroine it can be said that she makes the most of his vision and dominates his drama of transatlantic relations. This young woman is his favorite American type, appearing in his work time and again under various names and in various situations that can be taken as so many stages in her career. Hence it is in the line of her development that we must study her. Her case involves a principle of growth which is not to be completely grasped until she has assumed her final shape.

This heroine, too, is cast in the role, so generic to James, of the "passionate pilgrim," whose ordinary features are those of the "good American bewildered in the presence of the European order." But bewilderment is not a lasting motive in this heroine's conduct; unlike most of her fellow-pilgrims in James's novels, she soon learns how to adjust European attitudes to the needs of her personality. Where she excels is in her capacity to plunge into experience without paying the usual Jamesian penalty for such daring—the penalty being either the loss of one's moral balance or the recoil into a state of aggrieved innocence. She responds "magnificently" to the beauty of the old-world scene even while keeping a tight hold on her native virtue: the ethical stamina, good will, and inwardness of her own provincial background. And thus living up to her author's idea both of Europe and America, she is able to mediate, if not wholly to resolve, the conflict between the two cultures, between innocence and experience, between the sectarian code of the fathers and the more "civilized" though also more devious and dangerous code of the lovers. No wonder James commends her in terms that fairly bristle with heroic intentions and that in the preface to *The Wings of the Dove* he goes so far as to credit her with the great historic boon of being "that certain sort of young American," exceptionally endowed with "liberty of action, of choice, of appreciation, of contact . . . who is more the 'heir of all the ages' than any other young person whatsoever."

If James's relation to his native land is in question, then more is to be learned from this young woman's career than from any number of discursive statements quoted from his letters, essays, and autobiographies. "It's a complete fate being an American," he wrote. Yes, but what does this fate actually come to in his work? The answer, it seems to me, is mostly given in his serial narrative of the heiress of all the ages.

The initial assignment of this heroine is to reconnoiter the scene rather than take possession of it. As yet she is not recognized as the legitimate heiress but merely as a candidate for the inheritance. Such is the part played by Mary Garland, for instance, a small-town girl from New England who herself feels the pull of the "great world" even as she tries to save her errant lover from its perils (*Roderick Hudson*, 1875). Daisy Miller, a young lady whose friends are distressed by the odd mixture of spontaneous grace, audacity, and puerility in her deportment, is also cast in this role, though with somewhat special and limited intentions. Bessie Alden (*An International Episode*, 1878), a more cultivated and socially entrenched figure than the famous Daisy, voyages to England—inevitably so—for the sake of enjoying its picturesque associations; and she is noteworthy as the first of the James girls to reap the triumph of turning down the proposal of an old-world aristocrat. But it is in Isabel Archer (*The Portrait of a Lady*) that we first encounter this heroine in a truly pivotal position, comprising the dramatic consequences of a conflict not merely of manners but of morals as well. In Isabel her heretofore scattered traits are unified and corrected in the light of James's growing recognition of the importance of her claims. Two decades later, at the time when his writing had settled into the so portentously complex style of his ultimate period, she reappears as the masterful though stricken Milly Theale of *The Wings of the Dove* and as the impeccable Maggie Verver of *The Golden Bowl,* to whom all shall be given. These last displays of her are by far the most accomplished, for in them her function as "princess" and "heiress" is fully defined and affirmed.

The evolution of our heroine thus gives us the measure of James's progressively rising estimate of that American fate to the account of which he devoted the greater part of his work. The account opens with the simple, almost humble, instances of Mary Garland and Daisy Miller, who are baffled and shamed by Europe, and closes with the "prodigious" success of Maggie Verver, to whom Europe offers itself as a dazzling and inexhaustible opportunity. What is the heiress, then, if not a character-image of aggrandizement on every level of meaning and existence? She is that in her own right, as the representative American mounting "Europe's lighted and decorated stage"; but she also serves James as the objective equivalent of his own increase and expansion as man and artist. This is all the more striking when we consider that both author and heroine entered upon their careers under seemingly inauspicious circumstances. At the start they are beset by the traditional scruples of their race, by fits of enervation and recurrent feelings of inferiority; yet as both mature he achieves a creative dignity and consciousness of well-nigh lordly dimensions, while she comes to value herself and to be valued by the world at large as the personage appointed by history to inherit the bounty of the ages. Francis Fergusson has aptly summed up this entire process of growth in remarking that James "developed a society manner into a grand manner much as he developed a rich American girl into a larger, sober, Bérénice-like stage queen."

Such exceptional prosperity is hardly to be explained in terms of individual aptitude alone. Certain large conditions make it possible, such as America's precipitant rise as a national power in the late nineteenth century; its enhanced self-knowledge and self-confidence; and, more particularly, the avid desire of its upper classes to obtain forthwith the rewards and prerogatives of high civilization. The truth is that for qualities of a surpassingly bourgeois and imperial order James's heiress is without parallel in American fiction. Note that this millionaire's daughter is an heiress in moral principle no less than in material fact, and that James, possessed of a firmer faith in the then existing structure of society than most novelists and wholly sincere in his newly gained worldliness, tends to identify her moral with her material superiority.* Yet in

---

* Some critics writing about James in the early 1930's sought to put him in line with the leftist trend of the times. This sort of intention is evident in Robert Cantwell's several essays of that period and to a lesser extent in Stephen Spender's study, *The Destructive Element.* These critics overlook, it seems to me, the depth of the conservative idea in James, and that is why they are forced to exaggerate the meaning of novels like *The Ivory Tower* and *The Princess Casamassima.* Even though in the latter the atmosphere of class conflict is genuine enough, its revolutionary theme cannot be taken at face value. For imbedded in this novel is the more familiar theme of the passionate pilgrim—the pilgrim being the hero, Hyacinth Robinson, who sees the "immeasurable misery of the people" but who also sees, even more clearly and passionately, "all that has been, as it were, rescued and redeemed from it: the treasures, the felicities, the splendors, the successes

54

the long run she cannot escape the irony—the inner ambiguity—of her status. For her wealth is at once the primary source of her so lavishly pictured "greatness" and "liberty" and the source of the evil she evokes in others. There is no ignoring the consideration, however, that in the case of the heiress, as in the case of most of James's rich Americans, money is in a sense but the prerequisite of moral delicacy. What with her "higher interests" and pieties, the rigor of her conscience and the nicety of her illusions, what is she really if not a graduate of the school of Boston Transcendentalism? Her author's imagination operated according to the law of the conversion of the lower into the higher, and by means of this ideal logic his heroine's debut in the "social successful worldly world" is transformed into a kind of spiritual romance. What James knew best of all is, of course, how to take things immensely for granted; and not to appreciate the wonder of his beguilement is to miss the poetry, the story, the very life of his fictions.

To grasp the national-cultural values implicit in the progress of his heroine is to be done once and for all with

---

of the world"; and in the end, when the final choice is put to him, he takes his stand not with the people but with the "world" resting upon their misery. Thus Robinson is enticed by the same image that draws the Jamesian Americans to Europe. The one variation is that he constructs this image out of class rather than national or, so to speak, hemispheric differences.

So far as the political estimate of James is concerned, one cannot but agree with Joseph Warren Beach that he is basically a "gentleman of cultivated and conservative, not to say, reactionary instinct, who will generally be found to favor the same line of conduct as that favored by the ecclesiastical and civil law, as far as the law goes" (*The Method of Henry James*). So blunt a characterisation is likely to offend the James-cultists, but I think it can stand so long as we take it in a strictly political sense, not as a judgment of his moral realism. On that score Spender is closer to the truth in observing that James "saw through the life of his age" but that he "cherished the privilege that enabled him to see through it."

the widely held assumption that to James the country of his birth always signified failure and sterility. Edmund Wilson is surely right in contending that it is America which really "gets the better of it in Henry James." Such an interpretation is consistent with his return to the theme of the heiress at the turn of the century, with his honorific treatment of her, his enamored tone and laudatory report of her aims and prospects—her aims and prospects being not merely those of a typical Jamesian aspirant but of an American emissary endowed with a character "intrinsically and actively ample . . . reaching southward, westward, anywhere, everywhere." As the years passed James's awareness of the American stake in the maintenance of civilization grew increasingly positive and imposing. In his later writings old Europe serves once more as the background for young America, and his restored interest in the nuclear fable of the passionate pilgrim is now worked out on a more ambitious scale and with more intricate artistic intentions. His last great novels are remarkable, too, for the resurgence in them of that native idealism—that "extraordinary good faith"—the effect of which in his early fiction was to link him with the classic masters of American literature. In *The Wings of the Dove, The Ambassadors,* and *The Golden Bowl* the motives and standards of this idealism are applied to the mixed disorder and splendor of the "great world," now no longer simply admired from afar but seen from within.

But the question whether the ultimate loyalty of James is claimed by Europe or America is hardly as meaningful as it has appeared to some of his interpreters. For actually his valuations of Europe and America are not the polar opposites but the two commanding centers of his work—the contending sides whose relation is adjusted so as to make mutual assimilation feasible. It is the only means by which the Jamesian idea of heritage can be brought to fruition. What his detractors can never forgive him, however, is his bursting the bounds of that autarchic Americanism of which Whitman is the chief exponent. Never having fallen into the habit of "glowing belligerently with one's country," he is able to invest his characters with an historic mission and propel them into spheres of experience as yet closed to them at home. They are the people named as the Ambassadors—and the nationalist critics who make so much of his expatriation should be reminded that there is a world of difference between the status of an ambassador and the status of a fugitive.

James's all-inclusive choice is dramatised in his recurrent story of the marriage of an eminent new-world bride to an equally eminent old-world groom. The marriage is symbolic of the reconciliation of their competing cultures; and if it sometimes turns out badly, as in *The Portrait of a Lady*, or if it fails to come off altogether, as in *The Wings of the Dove*, James still holds fast to his scheme, continuing his experiments in matchmaking till finally, in *The Golden Bowl*, all the parts fall into their proper place, the marriage is consummated and bears luxurious fruit. Observe, though, that this happy ending is postponed again and again until the American wife, in the person of Maggie Verver, has established herself as the ruling member of the alliance.

The advancement of this heroine takes on historical form against the period background of the American female's rise to a position of cultural prestige and authority. She it was who first reached out for the "consummations and amenities" of life while her male relatives were still earnestly engaged in procuring its "necessities and preparations." No wonder W. D. Howells declared that "the prosperity of our fiction resides in the finer female sense." Now James's so-called feminine orientation is to be explained partly by this social fact and partly by his instinct, the most exquisite possible, for private relations and for their latent refinement of fact and taste. So estranged was he from typical masculine interests that he could not but fall back more and more on the subject of marriage, a subject dominated, in his treatment of it, by

57

the "social" note and meeting the "finer female sense" on its own preferred ground.* Moreover, he could have found no better framework of realistic detail for his picture of "young American innocence transplanted to European air." And if his stories of marriage are mostly stories, as he himself once put it, about "very young women, who, affected with a certain high lucidity, thereby become characters," it is because all the conditions of his art made for such a choice.

His male figures are, generally speaking, to be identified with his less masterful side, with the negative component of his sense of experience and the masochistic tendency to refuse the natural gifts of life. It is in deviating from this code of refusal that Roderick Hudson goes to pieces. In *The Ambassadors* Lambert Strether learns the lesson of *not* refusing, but his adventure in Paris gains its point from the sheer process of his learning that lesson rather than from his application of it. Nor can one overlook the repeated appearance in James of certain sad and uncertain young men who vie with each other in devising painfully subtle motives for renouncing their heart's desire once it is within their grasp. One such specimen is the young man (Bernard Longmore in *Madame de Mauves*) who is revolted by the idea of making love to the woman whose happiness he tries to save. Another is the incredibly appealing though emotionally dense Mr. Wendover, who has "no more physical personality than a consulted thermometer" and who, courting the girl he

---

* In *The Point of View,* a story published in the early 8o's, James inserts the following ironic reference to himself into the Paris-bound letter of a French visitor to New York: "They have a novelist here with pretensions to literature, who writes about the chase for the husband and the adventures of the rich Americans in our corrupt old Europe, where their primeval candor puts the Europeans to shame. *C'est proprement écrit;* but it's terribly pale." In later years he would hardly have enjoyed any such ironic play at his own expense, for with age self-depreciation gave way to portentousness in his estimate of himself.

loves with more propriety than imagination, fails her when she needs him most (*A London Life*). In point of fact, the heiress is the one native Jamesian who knows exactly what she wants. She, too, is confronted, to be sure, with "beautiful difficulties," but they are never of the kind that spring from some crucial frustration or of the kind that can be translated into some moral issue, which is then to be carefully isolated and solved in a chessboard fashion. In her case the "beautiful difficulties" spring out of her very search for self-fulfillment and impetuosity in "taking full in the face the whole assault of life."

It is with a bright and sudden flutter of self-awareness that Mary Garland reveals, in a brief passage of dialogue, the state of mind of the heiress as she sets out to meet her fate. The occasion for it is a night scene in *Roderick Hudson*, when Mary confesses to Rowland Mallet that her stay in Italy has induced a change in her conception of life:

Mary: "At home . . . things don't speak to us of enjoyment as they do here. Here it's such a mixture; one doesn't know what to believe. Beauty stands here—beauty such as this night and this place and all this sad strange summer have been so full of—and it penetrates one's soul and lodges there and keeps saying that man wasn't made, as we think at home, to struggle so much and to miss so much, but to ask of life as a matter of course some beauty and some charm. This place has destroyed any scrap of consistency that I ever possessed, but even if I must say something sinful I love it!"

Rowland: "If it's sinful I absolve you—in so far as I have power. We should not be able to enjoy, I suppose, unless we could suffer, and in anything that's worthy of the name of experience—that experience which is the real *taste* of life, isn't it?—the mixture is of the finest and subtlest."

The pathos of this dialogue is the pathos of all the buried things in the American past it recalls us to. It recalls us, moreover, to one of the most telling and precise relations in our literature, that of the early James to

Hawthorne.* Consider how this relation is at once contained and developed in Mary's vision of what life holds for those bold enough to ask for it as a matter of course "some beauty and some charm." For Mary is essentially a figure from a novel such as *The Blithedale Romance* or *The Marble Faun* brought forward into a later age; and because of the shift of values that has occurred in the meantime, she is able to express in a mundane fashion those feelings and sentiments that in Hawthorne are still somewhat hidden and only spoken of with a semiclerical quaver, as if from under a veil. In Mary's confession the spectral consciousness of the perils of beauty, of the evil it hides, is at long last being exorcised, the mind is being cleared of its home-grown fears and mystifications. The reality of experience can no longer be resisted: "Even if I say something sinful I love it!" And having said it, she is absolved of her "sin" by Rowland, who in this scene is manifestly acting for the author. It is Rowland, too, who describes experience as the "real *taste* of life," thus disclosing its innermost Jamesian sense. For in this sense of it the idea of experience is emptied of its more ordinary meanings, of empirical reference, and made to correspond to pure consummation, to that "felt felicity" so often invoked by James, to something lovingly selected or distilled from life—all of which is perfectly in line with the indicated function of the heiress as the prime consumer of the resources, material and spiritual, of both the Old and the New World. And though it is not within the power of even this superior brand of experience to exempt one from suffering, still the risk is well worth taking so long as "the mixture is of the finest and subtlest."

* Among the first to notice the connection was William James. In 1870 he wrote to his brother: "It tickled my national feeling not a little to note the resemblance of Hawthorne's style to yours and Howells's. . . . That you and Howells, with all the models in English literature to follow, should involuntarily have imitated (as it were) this American, seems to point to the existence of some real mental American quality."

But in Mary the ferment of experience is as yet more potential than actual. At this stage James is already sure of his heroine's integrity and liveliness of imagination, knowing that in this fine flower of a provincial culture he had gotten hold of an historical prodigy admirably suited to his purpose as a novelist. He is still doubtful, however, of her future, uncertain as to the exact conditions of her entry into the "great world" and of the mutual effect thus created. Daisy Miller and Bessie Alden represent his further experiments with her character. Daisy's social adventures make for a superb recreation of manners and tones and contrasts and similitudes. Spontaneity is her principal quality—a quality retained by the heiress through all her mutations and invariably rendered as beautifully illustrative of the vigor and innocence of the national spirit. But Daisy is altogether the small-town, the average American girl; and by virtue of this fact she lays bare the lowly origin of the heiress in the undifferentiated mass of the new-world democracy. Winterbourne, Daisy's admirer and critic, observes that "she and her mamma have not yet risen to the stage—what shall I call it?—of culture, at which the idea of catching a count or a *marchese* begins." Bessie, on the other hand, seizes upon this conception only to rise above it. This "Bostonian nymph who rejects an English duke" combines the primal sincerity of her forebears with a Jamesian sensitivity to the "momentos and reverberations of greatness" in the life of ancient aristocracies—and this amalgam of values proves to be beyond the comprehension of Lord Lambeth's simple matter-of-fact mind. Bessie's behavior was resented, of course, by English readers, just as Daisy's was resented by American readers. But the so-challenged author, far from being flustered by the protests that reached him, took it all in with gloating satisfaction, delighted by the contrast, with its "dramas upon dramas . . . and innumerable points of view," thus brought to light. He felt that the emotion of the public vindicated his faith in the theme of the "international situation."

As the 1870's come to a close, James is done with the preliminary studies of his heroine. Now he undertakes to place her in a longer narrative—*The Portrait of a Lady*—the setting and action of which are at last commensurate with the "mysterious purposes" and "vast designs" of her character. In the preface to the New York edition (written nearly a quarter of a century later) he recalls that the conception of a "certain young woman affronting her destiny had begun with being all my outfit for the large building of the novel"; and he reports that in its composition he was faced with only one leading question: "What will she 'do'?" But this is mainly a rhetorical question, for naturally "the first thing she'll do will be to come to Europe—which in fact will form, and all inevitably, no small part of her principal adventure." *The Portrait* is by far the best novel of James's early prime, bringing to an end his literary apprenticeship and establishing the norms of his world. Its author has not yet entirely divorced himself from Victorian models in point of structure, and as a stylist he is still mindful of the reader's more obvious pleasure, managing his prose with an eye to outward as well as inward effects. It is a lucid prose, conventional yet free, marked by aphoristic turns of phrase and by a kind of intellectual gaiety in the formulation of ideas. There are few signs as yet of that well-nigh metaphysical elaboration of the sensibility by which he is to become known as one of the foremost innovators in modern writing.

Isabel Archer is a young lady of an Emersonian cast of mind, but her affinity as a fictional character is rather with those heroines of Turgenev in whose nature an extreme tenderness is conjoined with unusual strength of purpose.* No sooner does Isabel arrive at the country-

---

* The influence may well be conscious in this case, though in the preface to the novel James admits to being influenced by the Russian novelist only on the technical plane, with respect

62

house of her uncle Mr. Touchett, an American banker residing in England, then everyone recognizes her for what she is—"a delicate piece of human machinery." Her cousin Ralph questions his mother: "Who is this rare creature, and what is she? Where did you find her?" "I found her," she replies, "in an old house at Albany, sitting in a dreary room on a rainy day. . . . She didn't know she was bored, but when I told her she seemed grateful for the hint. . . . I thought she was meant for something better. It occurred to me it would be a kindness to take her about and introduce her to the world." The American Cinderella thus precipitated from the town of Albany into the "great world" knows exactly what she must look forward to. "To be as happy as possible," she confides in Ralph, "that's what I came to Europe for." It is by no means a simple answer. On a later and more splendid occasion it is to be repeated by Maggie Verver, who proclaims her faith, even as the golden bowl crashes to the ground, in a "happiness without a hole in it . . . the golden bowl as it *was* to have been . . . the bowl with all our happiness in it, the bowl without a crack in it." This is the crowning illusion and pathos, too, of the heiress, that she believes such happiness to be attainable, that money can buy it and her mere good faith can sustain it. And even when eventually her European entanglements open her eyes to the fact that virtue and experience are not so charmingly compatible after all, that the Old World has a fierce energy of its own and that its "tone of time" is often pitched in a sinister key, she still persists in her belief that this same world will yield her a richly personal happiness, proof against the evil spawned by others less fortunate than herself; and this belief is all the more expressive because it is wholly of a piece with the psychology of the heiress as a national

to the manner of placing characters in fiction. James's critical essays abound with favorable references to Turgenev, whose friendship he cultivated in Paris and of whom he invariably spoke with enthusiasm.

type. The ardor of Americans in pursuing happiness as a personal goal is equalled by no other people, and when it eludes them none are so hurt, none so shamed. Happiness, one might say, is really their private equivalent of such ideals as progress and universal justice. They take for granted, with a faith at once deeply innocent and deeply presumptuous, that they deserve nothing less and that to miss it is to miss life itself.

The heiress is not to be humbled by the tests to which life in Europe exposes her. The severer the test the more intense the glow of her spirit. Is she not the child, as Isabel proudly declares, of that "great country which stretches beyond the rivers and across the prairies, blooming and smiling and spreading, till it stops at the blue Pacific! A strong, sweet, fresh odour seems to rise from it. . . ." The Emersonian note is sounded again and again by Isabel. She is truly the Young American so grandly pictured by the Concord idealist in his essay of that title, the Young American bred in a land "offering opportunity to the human mind not known in any other region" and hence possessed of an "organic simplicity and liberty, which, when it loses its balance, redresses itself presently. . . ." Witness the following passage of character-analysis, with its revelation of Isabel's shining beneficient Emersonianism:

Every now and then Isabel found out she was wrong, and then she treated herself to a week of passionate humility. After that she held her head higher than ever; for it was of no use, she had an unquenchable desire to think well of herself. She had a theory that it was only on this condition that life was worth living: that one should be of the best, should be conscious of a fine organization . . . *should move in a realm of light, of natural wisdom, of happy impulse, of inspiration fully chronic. It was almost as unnecessary to cultivate doubt of oneself as to cultivate doubt of one's best friend.* . . . The girl had a certain nobleness of imagination which rendered her a good many services and played her a good many tricks. She spent half her time in thinking of beauty, and bravery, and magnanimity; *she had a fixed determination to regard the world as a place of brightness, of free ex-*

64

pansion, of irresistible action; she thought it would be detesta-
ble to be afraid or ashamed. (Italics not in the original.)

Still more revealing is the exchange between Isabel and the thoroughly Europeanised Madame Merle on the subject of the individual's capacity for self-assertion in the face of outward circumstances:

Madame Merle: "When you have lived as long as I, you will see that every human being has his shell, that you must take the shell into account. By the shell I mean the whole envelope of circumstances. There is no such thing as an isolated man or woman; we're each of us made up of a cluster of circumstances. What do you call one's self? Where does it begin? Where does it end? It overflows into everything that belongs to me—and then it flows back again. I know that a large part of myself is in the dresses I choose to wear. I have a great respect for *things!*"

Isabel: "I don't agree with you. . . . I think just the other way. I don't know whether I succeed in expressing myself, but I know that nothing else expresses me. Nothing that belongs to me is a measure of me; on the contrary, it's a limit, a barrier, and a perfectly arbitrary one." *

In *The Portrait* James is still hesitating between the attitude of Madame Merle and that of Isabel, and his irony is provoked by the excessive claims advanced by both sides. But in years to come he is to be drawn more and more to the "European" idea of the human self, his finer discriminations being increasingly engaged by the "envelope of circumstances" in which it is contained.

Isabel is above all a young lady of principles, and her most intimate decisions are ruled by them. In refusing the proposal of the grandiose Lord Warburton, she wonders what ideal aspiration or design upon fate or con-

---

* Note the close parallel between Isabel's reply to Madame Merle and the Emersonian text. "You think me the child of my circumstances: I make my circumstances. Let any thought or motive of mine be different from what they are, the difference will transform my condition and economy. . . . You call it the power of circumstance, but it is the power of me." (*The Transcendentalist*)

ception of happiness prompts her to renounce such a chance for glamor and worldly satisfaction. Never had she seen a "personage" before, as there were none in her native land; of marriage she had been accustomed to think solely in terms of character—"of what one likes in a gentleman's mind and in his talk . . . hitherto her visions of a completed life had concerned themselves largely with moral images—things as to which the question would be whether they pleased her soul." But if an aristocratic marriage is not to Isabel's liking, neither is the strictly hometown alternative of marrying a business man. The exemplary Gaspar Goodwood, who owns a cotton-mill and is the embodiment of patriotic virtue, likewise fails to win her consent.—"His jaw was too square and grim, and his figure too straight and stiff; these things suggested a want of easy adaptability to some of the occasions of life."

Isabel having so far lacked the requisite fortune to back up her assumption of the role of the heiress, her cousin Ralph provides what is wanting by persuading his dying father to leave her a large sum of money. "I should like to make her rich," Ralph declares. "What do you mean by rich?" "I call people rich when they are able to gratify their imagination." Thus Isabel enters the uppermost circle of her author's hierarchy, the circle of those favored few who, unhampered by any material coercion, are at once free to make what they can of themselves and to accept the fullest moral responsibility for what happens to them in consequence. Now the stage is set for the essential Jamesian drama of free choice. In this novel, however, the transcendent worth of such freedom is not yet taken for granted as it is in *The Wings of the Dove* and *The Golden Bowl*. There is the intervention, for instance, of the lady-correspondent Henrietta Stackpole, who is no passionate pilgrim but the mouthpiece, rather, of popular Americanism. It is she who questions Isabel's future on the ground that her money will work against her by bolstering her romantic inclinations. Henrietta is little more than a fictional convenience used to furnish the story with comic relief; but at this juncture of the plot she becomes the agent of a profound criticism aimed, in the last analysis, at James himself, at his own tendency to romanticise the values to which privilege lays claim. And what Henrietta has to say is scarcely in keeping with her habitual manner of the prancing female journalist. Characteristically enough, she begins by remarking that she has no fear of Isabel turning into a sensual woman; the peril she fears is of a different nature:

"The peril for you is that you live too much in the world of your own dreams—you are not enough in contact with reality —with the toiling, striving, suffering, I may even say, sinning world that surrounds you. You are too fastidious, you have too many graceful illusions. Your newly-acquired thousands will shut you up more and more in the society of selfish and heartless people, who will be interested in keeping up those illusions. . . . You think, furthermore, that you can lead a romantic life, that you can live by pleasing others and pleasing yourself. You will find you are mistaken. Whatever life you lead, you must put your soul into it—to make any sort of success of it; and from the moment you do that it ceases to be romance, I assure you; it becomes reality! . . . you think we can escape disagreeable duties by taking romantic views—that is your great illusion, my dear."

The case against the snobbish disposition of the Jamesian culture-seekers and their overestimation of the worldly motive has seldom been so shrewdly and clearly stated. But Isabel is not especially vulnerable to criticism of this sort. It is only in her later incarnations that the heiress succumbs more and more to precisely the illusions of which Henrietta gives warning—so much so that in the end, when Maggie Verver appears on the scene, the life she leads may be designated, from the standpoint of the purely social analyst, as a romance of bourgeois materialism, the American romance of newly got wealth divesting itself of its plebeian origins in an ecstasy of refinement! Henrietta's words, moreover, are meant to prefigure the tragedy of Isabel's marriage to Gilbert Osmond, an Italianate American, virtually a European, whom she takes to be what he is not—a decent compromise between the moral notions of her American background and the glamor of the European foreground. Osmond, whose special line is a dread of vulgarity, employs a kind of sincere cunning in presenting himself to Isabel as the most fastidious gentleman living, concerned above all with making his life a work of art and resolved, since he could never hope to attain the status he actually deserved, "not to go in for honors." The courtship takes place in Rome and in Florence, where Isabel is swayed by her impression of Osmond as a "quiet, clever, distinguished man, strolling on a moss-grown terrace above the sweet Val d'Arno . . . the picture was not brilliant, but she liked its lowness of tone, and the atmosphere of summer twilight that pervaded it. . . . It seemed to speak of a serious choice, a choice between things of a shallow and things of a deep interest; of a lonely, studious life in a lovely land." But the impression is false. Only when it is too late does she learn that he had married her for her money with the connivance of Madame Merle, his former mistress, who had undertaken to influence her in his behalf. This entrapment of Isabel illustrates a recurrent formula of James's fiction. The person springing the trap is almost invariably driven by mercenary motives, and, like Osmond, is capable of accomplishing his aim by simulating a sympathy and understanding that fascinate the victim and render her (or him) powerless.* Osmond still retains some features of the old-fashioned villain, but his successors are gradually freed from the encumbrances of melodrama.

---

* It seems to me that this brand of evil has much in common with the "unpardonable sin" by which Hawthorne was haunted —the sin of *using* other people, of "violating the sanctity of a human heart." Chillingsworth in *The Scarlet Letter* is essentially this type of sinner, and so is Miriam's model in *The Marble Faun*. In James, however, the evil characters have none of the Gothic *mystique* which is to be found in Hawthorne. Their motives are transparent.

Merton Densher (*The Wings of the Dove*) and Prince Amerigo (*The Golden Bowl*) are men of grace and intelligence, whose wicked behavior is primarily determined by the situation in which they find themselves.

Osmond reacts to the Emersonian strain in Isabel as to a personal offence. He accuses her of wilfully rejecting traditional values and of harboring sentiments "worthy of a radical newspaper or a Unitarian preacher." And she, on her part, discovers that his fastidiousness reduced itself to a "sovereign contempt for every one but some two or three or four exalted people whom he envied, and for everything but half-a-dozen ideas of his own . . . he pointed out to her so much of the baseness and shabbiness of life . . . but this base, ignoble world, it appeared, was after all what one was to live for; one was to keep it forever in one's eye, in order, not to enlighten, or convert, or redeem, but to extract from it some recognition of one's superiority." Isabel's notion of the aristocratic life is "simply the union of great knowledge with great liberty," whereas for Osmond it is altogether a "thing of forms," an attitude of conscious calculation. His esteem for tradition is boundless; if one was so unfortunate as not to be born to an illustrious tradition, then "one must immediately proceed to make it."* A

---

* The significance of Osmond's character has generally been underrated by the critics of James. For quite apart from his more personal traits (such as his depravity, which is a purely novelistic element), he is important as a cultural type in whom the logic of "traditionalism" is developed to its furthest limits. As a national group the American intellectuals suffer from a sense of inferiority toward the past, and this residue of "colonial" feeling is also to be detected in those among them who raise the banner of tradition. It is shown in their one-sided conformity to the idea of tradition, in their readiness to inflate the meanings that may be derived from it. Their tendency is to take literally what their European counterparts are likely to take metaphorically and imaginatively. My idea is that James tried to overcome this bias which he suspected in himself by objectifying it in the portrait of Osmond. To this day, however, the shadow of Gilbert Osmond falls on many a

sense of darkness and suffocation takes hold of Isabel as her husband's rigid system closes in on her. She believes that there can be no release from the bondage into which she had fallen and that only through heroic suffering is its evil to be redeemed. On this tragic note the story ends.

Yet the heiress is not to be turned aside from her quest by such inevitable encounters with the old evils of history. On the lighted stage the bridegroom still awaits his new-world bride.

In few of his full-length novels is James so consummately in control of his method of composition as in *The Wings of the Dove* and *The Golden Bowl.* It is a method all scenic and dramatic, of an "exquisite economy" in the architectonic placing of incidents, which eliminates any "going behind or telling about the figures" save as they themselves accomplish it. Indulgence in mere statement is banned; the motto is: *represent, convert, dramatize.* By means of this compositional economy the story is so organized that it seems to tell itself, excluding all material not directly bearing on the theme. This despite the "complication of innuendo and associative reference," as William James called it, by which the author communicates the vital information needed to understand the action. Complications of this sort so confuse some readers that they see nothing but surplusmatter and digression where, in fact, everything is arranged in the most compact order. Nor is the occasional wordiness and vagueness of James's prose germane to our judgment of his novelistic structure. Even the thoughts of his characters are reproduced along exclusive rather than inclusive lines, as in *The Golden Bowl,* where the interior monologues of Maggie and the Prince are in reality a kind of speech which no one happens to overhear, show-

---

page of American writing whose author—whether critic, learned poet, or academic "humanist"—presents himself, with all the exaggerated zeal and solemnity of a belated convert, as a spokesman of tradition.

ing none of the rich incoherence, haphazardness, and latitude of Joyce's rendering of the private mind, for example.

The principle of free association is incompatible with the Jamesian technique, which is above all a technique of exclusion. One can best describe it, it seems to me, as the fictional equivalent of the poetic modes evolved by modern poets seeking to produce a "pure poetry." In this sense the later James has more in common with a poet like Mallarmé than with novelists like Joyce and Proust, whose tendency is to appropriate more and more material and to assimilate to their medium even such non-fictional forms as the poem and the essay. In Proust the specific experience is made use of to launch all sorts of generalisations, to support, that is, his innumerable analyses—by turn poetic and essayistic—of memory, love, jealousy, the nature of art, etc. In Joyce this impulse to generalization finds other outlets, such as the investing of the specific experience with mythic associations that help us to place it within the pattern of human recurrence and typicality. James tightens where Joyce and Proust loosen the structure of the novel. In their hands the novel takes on encyclopedic dimensions, surrendering its norms and imperialistically extending itself, so to speak, to absorb all literary genres. It might be claimed, in fact, that *the novel as they write it ceases to be itself, having been transformed into a comprehensive work from which none of the resources of literature are excluded.* Not that they abandon the principle of selection; the point is rather that they select material to suit their desire for an unrestricted expansion of the medium, whereas James selects with a view to delimiting the medium and defining its proper course. He confirms, as very few novelists do, Goethe's observation that the artistic effect requires a closed space. It is true that at bottom it is culture and the history of culture which constitute the inner theme of all three writers, but while Joyce and Proust express it by continually revealing its universality, James expresses

71

it by limiting himself, through an extraordinary effort of aesthetic calculation, to its particularity.

One need not go so far as to say that the formal character of the Jamesian novel is determined by its social character in order to emphasize the close relation between the two. Both manifest the same qualities of particularity and exclusiveness. But why, it might be asked, is Proust's work so different in form, given the fact that he, too, is drawn by the resplendent image of the "great world" and, presumably, is quite as responsive to some of the values attributed to James? The answer would be that even on this ground the American and the French novelist are more at variance than would seem at first glance.

Proust's picture of society contains elements of lyricism as well as elements of objective analysis. He is a more realistic painter of social manners than James, perhaps for the reason that he permits no ethical issues to intervene between him and the subject, approaching the world *ab initio* with the tacit assumption that ethics are irrelevant to its functions. By comparison James is a traditional moralist whose insight into experience turns on his judgment of conduct. If sometimes, as in *The Golden Bowl,* we are made to feel that he is withholding judgment or judging wrongly, that may be because he is either conforming, or appears to conform, to certain moral conventions of the world's making by which it manages to flatter itself. In Proust such conventions are brought out into the open, but not for purposes of moral judgment. The sole morality of which the protagonist of his novel is conscious grows out of the choice he faces between two contrary ideals. He must decide whether to pursue the art of life or the life of art, and the novel can be said to be an epical autobiography of his effort to come to a decision. But it is not until the end-volume that the world is finally renounced; and through a kind of optical illusion induced by the novel's astonishing unfoldment, we seem to participate in this renunciation of the world at the precise moment when its alternative—*i.e.*, the work of art—actually comes into being, or, more accurately, is at last fully realized. Since in this work the world is overcome only after it has been possessed, the unity of life and art is affirmed in it despite the author's attempt to divorce them by closing with a purely subjective account of the artistic process. No matter what Proust intended this account to mean, taken in its context it affects us as an ironic expression of the artist's triumph over his material, a mocking valediction addressed to that recalcitrant angel—the objective spirit of reality—with whom the artist grappled through the long night of creation and, having gotten the better of him, can now treat with disdain.

But if in Proust art and life are unified by the contradiction between them, in James they are initially combined in his root-idea of experience. His passionate pilgrims, such as the heiress, are driven, despite all vacillations and retractions, by their need to master the world (which is identified with experience and the "real *taste* of life"), and in art they recognize the means by which the world becomes most richly aware of itself. As Americans they have come to it so belatedly that they can ill afford either the spiritual luxury or spiritual desperation of looking beyond it. This is the reason, I think, that except for the early example of *Roderick Hudson* and later of *The Tragic Muse,* the theme of art and artists enters significantly and independently only into some of James's short stories, in which he deals not with his representative figures but with his own case as a professional writer somewhat estranged from society by his devotion to his craft. Though these stories testify to the artistic idealism of their author, they can scarcely be taken as a serious challenge to the authority of the world.

Now at this point it should be evident that James's inability to overcome the world, in the sense that most European writers of like caliber overcome it, is due not to his being too much of it, but, paradoxically enough, to his being too little of it. And for that the explanation must be sought in his origins. For he approaches the world with certain presumptions of piety that clearly derive from the semireligious idealism of his family background and, more generally, from the early traditions and faith of the American community. But in James this idealism and faith undergo a radical change, in that they are converted to secular ends. Thus one might venture the speculation that his worldly-aesthetic idea of an elite is in some way associated, however remotely and unconsciously, with the ancestral-puritan idea of the elect; hence the ceremoniousness and suggestions of ritual in the social display of a novel like *The Golden Bowl*. So with the ancestral ideas of sin and grace. Is it not possible to claim that the famous Jamesian refinement is a trait in which the vision of an ideal state is preserved —the state of grace to be achieved here and now through mundane and aesthetic means? It is the vision by which Milly Theale is transported as she rests in her Venetian garden—the vision of "never going down, of remaining aloft in the divine dustless air, where she could but hear the plash of water against the stone." And through the same process, as I have already had occasion to remark, the fear of sin is translated in James into a revulsion, an exasperated feeling, almost morbid in its sensitiveness, against any conceivable crudity of scene or crudity of conduct.

Yet whatever the sources and implications of the social legend in James, I have no doubt that it enabled him as nothing else could to formulate his creative method and to remain true, even on his lower levels, to the essential mood and sympathy of his genius. There is an essay on Proust by Paul Valéry in which he speaks of the French novelist's capacity "to adapt the potentialities of his inner life" to the aim of expressing "one group of people . . . which calls itself Society," thus converting the picture of an avowedly superficial existence into a profound work. But I have always felt that what Valéry is saying in this essay could more appropriately be said about the later James than about Proust.—

The group which calls itself Society is composed of symbolic figures. Each of its members represents some abstraction. It is necessary that all the powers of this world should somewhere meet together; that *money* should converse with *beauty,* and *politics* become familiar with *elegance;* that *letters* and *birth* grow friendly and serve each other tea. . . . Just as a bank-note is only a slip of paper, so the member of society is a sort of fiduciary money made of living flesh. This combination is extremely favorable to the designs of a subtle novelist. . . . very great art, which is the art of simplified figures and the most pure types; in other words, of essences which permit the symmetrical and almost musical development of the consequences arising from a carefully isolated situation—such art involves the existence of a conventional milieu, where the language is adorned with veils and provided with limits, where *seeming* commands *being* and where *being* is held in a noble restraint which changes all of life into an opportunity to exercise presence of mind. (*A Tribute*)

This is, however, a peculiarly one-sided view of the Proustian scene, as Valéry allows himself to be carried away by the comparison between the old French literature of the Court and *À la recherche du temps perdu.* Proust balances his poetic appreciation of the Guermantes way with a more than sufficient realism in portraying the rages of Charlus, the passions of Saint-Loup, the schemes of Mme. Verdurin, Bloch, Morel, Jupien, etc.; nor is he averse to showing the pathological condition of that "group which calls itself Society"; he, too, is infected, after all, with the modern taste for excess, for speaking out with inordinate candor. The truth is that it is in James, rather than in Proust, that we often find it difficult to make certain of the real contours of *being* behind the smooth mask of *seeming.* It is *his* language which is "adorned with veils and provided with limits," and it is the conversation of *his* characters which is so allusive that it seems more to spare than to release the sense.

And Valéry continues: "After a new power has gained recognition, no great time passes before its representatives appear at the gatherings of society; and the movement of history is pretty well summarized by the successive admissions of different social types to the salons, hunts, marriages, and funerals of the supreme tribe of a nation." What an apt description of the rise of the heiress—of, say, Milly Theale entering a London drawing-room and being greeted by Lord Mark as the first woman of her time, or of Maggie Verver gravely telling the prince to whom she has just become engaged that he is an object of beauty, a *morceau du musée,* though of course she hasn't the least idea what it would cost her father to acquire him, and that together they shall possess the "world, the beautiful world!"

ATTITUDES TOWARD
HENRY JAMES

Henry James is at once the most and least appreciated figure in American writing. His authority as a novelist of unique quality and as an archetypal American has grown immeasurably in the years since his death, and in some literary circles his name has of late been turned into the password of a cult. But at the same time he is still regarded, in those circles that exert the major influence on popular education and intelligence, with the coldness and even derision that he encountered in the most depressed period of his career, when his public deserted him and he found himself almost alone.

To illustrate the extent to which he is even now misunderstood, let me cite the opening gambit of the section on James in *The College Book of American Literature,* a text currently used in many schools. "It is not certain that Henry James really belongs to American literature, for he was critical of America and admired Europe." The attitude so automatically expressed by the editors of this academic volume obviously borders on caricature. The responsibility for it, however, must be laid at the door of all those critics and historians who, in response to a deep anti-intellectual compulsion or at the service of some blindly nationalistic or social creed, are not content merely to say no to the claims made in James's behalf but must ever try to despoil him utterly. The strategy is simple: James was nothing but a self-deluded expatriate snob, a concocter of elegant if intricate trifles, a fugitive from "reality," etc., etc. Professor Pattee, a run-of-the-mill historian of American writing, permits himself the remark that James's novels "really accomplish nothing." Ludwig Lewisohn is likewise repelled by the novels—"cathedrals of frosted glass" he calls them; in his opinion only the shorter narratives are worth reading. In his *Main Currents* Parrington gives two pages to James as against eleven to James Branch Cabell, and he has the further temerity (and/or innocence) to round out his two pages by comparing James—much to his disadvantage, of course—to Sherwood Anderson. And Van Wyck Brooks does all he can, in *New England: Indian Summer,* to promote once more the notoriously low estimate of the later James to which he committed himself in *The Pilgrimage.* Brooks may well believe that the Jamesian attachment is to be counted among the fixed ideas of our native "coterie-writers"—and plainly the best cure for a fixed idea is to stamp on it.

This depreciation of James is prepared for by some of the leading assumptions of our culture. The attitude of Parrington, for example, is formed by the Populist spirit of the West and its open-air poetics, whereas that of Brooks is at bottom formed by the moralism of New England—a moralism to which he has reverted, even though in practice he applies it in a more or less impressionistic and sentimental manner, with all the vehemence of a penitent atoning for his backsliding in the past. And the difference between such typical attitudes is mainly this: that while Parrington—like Whitman and Mark Twain before him—rejects James entirely, Brooks at least recognizes the value and fidelity to life of his earlier novels. Yet if James can be named, in T. S. Eliot's phrase, "a positive continuator of the New England genius," then surely Brooks must be aware of it as well as any of us; for he is nothing if

78

not a pious servitor of this genius; after all, he, too, is a paleface. But still he scoffs at the more complex and, so to speak, ultimate James. And this Brooks does essentially for the same reasons, I think, that the Boston public of the 1870's scoffed at the works he now admits into his canon. We know that when the first of James's books appeared in America, they were actively disliked in Boston: Mrs. Fields (the wife of the publisher) relates that they were thought "self-conscious, artificial, and shallow." A like animus is now betrayed in Brooks's judgment of such novels as *The Spoils of Poynton, The Wings of the Dove,* and *The Golden Bowl*:

Magnificent pretensions, petty performances!—the fruits of an irresponsible imagination, of a deranged sense of values, of a mind working in a void, uncorrected by any clear conscious-ness of human cause and effect. (*The Pilgrimage of Henry James*)

There was scarcely enough substance in these great ghosts of novels. . . . What concerned him now was form, almost regardless of content, the problems of calculation and con-struction. . . . His American characters might be nobler, but, if the old world was corrupt, its glamor outweighed its cor-ruption in his mind . . . so that he later pictured people, actually base, as eminent, noble and great. (*New England: Indian Summer*)

What are such extreme statements if not critical ra-tionalizations of the original Boston prejudice? Brooks begins by magnifying the distinctions between James's early and late manner into an absolute contradiction, and ends by invoking the charge of degeneracy. But the fact is that the changes in James's work mark no such gap as Brooks supposes but are altogether implicit in the quality of his vision, flowing from the combined release and elabo-ration of his basic tendency. Moreover, these changes, far from justifying the charge of degeneracy, define for a good many of his readers the one salient example in our literature of a novelist who, not exhausted by his initial assertion of power, learned how to nourish his gifts and grow to full maturity. To me he is the only really fine

American writer of the nineteenth century who can truly be said to have mastered that "principle of growth," to the failure of which in our creative life Brooks has himself repeatedly called attention in his earlier preachments.

For what is to be admired in a late narrative like *The Wings of the Dove* is James's capacity to lift the nuclear theme of his first period—the theme of the American innocent's penetration into the "rich and deep and dark" hive of Europe—to a level of conscious experience and aesthetic possession not previously attained. James orders his world with consummate awareness in this narrative, applying successfully his favorite rule of an "exquisite economy" in composition. There are brilliant scenes in it of London and Venice, and strongly contrasted symbols of social glamor and decay; it is invigorated, too, by an unflagging realism in the plotting of act and motive and by the large movement of the characters. No literary standpoint that allows for the dismissal of this creation as a "petty performance" can possibly be valid. Is its heroine, Milly Theale, a character without reality? She remains in our mind, writes Edmund Wilson, "as a personality independent of the novel, the kind of personality, deeply felt, invested with poetic beauty and unmistakably individualized, which only the creators of the first rank can give life to."

James suffers from a certain one-sidedness, to be sure. This tends to throw off balance such readers as are unable to see it for what it is—the price he paid, given the circumstances of his career, for being faithful to his own genius. For James could continue to develop and sustain his "appeal to a high refinement and a handsome wholeness of effect" only through intensively exploiting his very limitations, through submitting himself to a process of creative yet cruel self-exaggeration. The strain shows in the stylization of his language, a stylization so rich that it turns into an intellectual quality of rare value, but which at times is apt to become overwrought and drop into unconscious parody. It is further shown in his obsessive refinement—a veritable delirium of refinement—which again serves at times to remove us from the actuality of the represented experience. This should be related to his all-too-persistent attempts, as Yvor Winters has observed, to make the sheer *tone* of speech and behavior "carry vastly more significance than is proper to it." It is true that, for instance, in novels like *The Sense of the Past* and *The Awkward Age,* he pushes his feelings for nuances and discriminations to an unworkable extreme. But such distortions, inflated into awful vices by his detractors, are of the kind which in one form or another not only James but most of the considerable modern artists are forced to cultivate as a means of coping with the negative environment that confines them. To regard such distortions as the traits of a willful coterie is utterly naive. They are the traits, rather, of an art which, if it is to survive at all in a society inimical to all interests that are pure, gratuitous, and without cash value, has no other recourse save constantly to "refine its singularities" and expose itself more and more to the ravages of an unmitigated individualism.

But in all this I do not mean to imply that I agree with those enthusiasts who see no moral defects whatever in James. From the viewpoint of social criticism, there is a good deal of justice in Ferner Nuhn's mordant analysis of *The Golden Bowl.** This novel is one of the much debated items in the James canon, for in it James applied his spellbinding powers as never before to the creation of a line of illusory value for his wealthy Americans in Europe and their sponging aristocratic friends with whom they conduct a romantic historical liaison. Not a few critics have been provoked by this quality of the novel. One instance is Stephen Spender, who, flying in the face of the Jamesian specifications, describes Prince Amerigo as "an unknown, well-bred scoundrel." Some have argued, weakly, I think, that the picture of the Ververs

---

* In his book, *The Wind Blows from the East,* 1942.

and their bought-and-paid-for Prince is to be taken in an ironical sense. In *Henry James: the Major Phase* F. O. Matthiessen takes the story as given, and his interpretation coincides in many respects with Ferner Nuhn's reading of it. I agree entirely with their approach, but one cannot go along with Matthiessen in his conclusion that the novel is "with all its magnificence . . . almost as hollow of real life as the chateaux that had risen along Fifth Avenue and that had also crowded out the old Newport world that James remembered." To say that *The Golden Bowl* is morally decadent is one thing, but to claim that for this reason it is empty of life and, by implication, an inferior work of art is something else again. To my mind, this is an example of moral over-reaction at the expense of literary judgment. I can think of other novels, say Dostoevsky's *The Possessed,* which are thoroughly distorted from the standpoint of any radical social morality but which are none the less supreme works of fiction. *The Golden Bowl* must be placed, I believe, among the half dozen great novels of American literature; there is one section in it—the second, third, and fourth chapters of the fifth "Book"—which for vividness, directness, and splendidly alive and spacious imagery is without counterpart in the American novel. Ferner Nuhn has defined *The Golden Bowl* as a dream story. He is right of course, since the indicated position of its characters and the idea they have of themselves are not in correspondence with reality. Yet as a dream story it is far from being a mere invention. It has the enormous vitality which springs from the actual dreamlife of a social class— a dream of the "loot of empire," an imperial dream full of "real" objects and "real" life. One can object to its content on ideological grounds, and on those grounds James is indeed vulnerable; but one cannot deny that it is historically meaningful and that it has interest and artistry and a kind of meditated though cruel beauty.

Furthermore, whatever one may think of the millionaire self-indulgence of the Ververs, this is a far cry from the charge that James's long exile put him into such a bad state that he could no longer distinguish between the noble and the base. This sort of charge is answered once and for all, it seems to me, by Stephen Spender in his study, *The Destructive Element*:

The morality of the heroes and heroines [in the last great novels] is to "suffer generously." What they have to suffer from is being more intelligent than the other characters. Also, there are no villains. It is important to emphasize this, because in these really savage novels the behavior of some of the characters is exposed in its most brutal form. But the wickedness of the characters lies primarily in their situation. Once the situation is provided, the actors cannot act otherwise. Their only compensation is that by the use of their intelligence, by their ability to understand, to love and to suffer, they may to some extent atone for the evil which is simply the evil of the modern world.

As against the sundry moralizers and nationalists who belittle James, there are the cultists who go to the other extreme in presenting him as a kind of culture-hero, an ideal master whose perfection of form is equaled by his moral insight and staunch allegiance to "tradition." This image is no doubt of consolatory value to some high-minded literary men. It contributes, however, to the misunderstanding of James, in that it is so impeccable, one might say transcendent, that it all but eliminates the contradictions in him—and in modern literature, which bristles with anxieties and ideas of isolation, it is above all the creativity, the depth and quality of the contradictions that a writer unites within himself, that gives us the truest measure of his achievement. And this is not primarily a matter of the solutions, if any, provided by the writer—for it is hardly the writer's business to stand in for the scientist or philosopher—but of his force and integrity in reproducing these contradictions as felt experience. Very few of us would be able to appreciate Dostoevsky, for instance, if we first had to accept his answer to the problem of the Christian man, or Proust if we first had to accept his answer to the problem of the artist. We appreciate these novelists because they employ imaginative means that convince us of the reality of their problems, which are not *necessarily* ours.

T. S. Eliot was surely right in saying that the soil of James's origin imparted a "flavor" that was "precisely improved and given its chance, not worked off" by his living in Europe. Now James differs radically in his contradictions from European novelists—that is why readers lacking a background in American or at least Anglo-Saxon culture make so little of him. And the chief contradiction is that his work represents a positive and ardent search for "experience" and simultaneously a withdrawal from it, or rather, a dread of approaching it in its natural state. Breaking sharply with the then still dominant American morality of abstention, he pictures "experience" as the "real taste of life," as a longed-for "presence" at once "vast, vague, and dazzling—an irradiation of light from objects undefined, mixed with the atmosphere of Paris and Venice." Nevertheless, to prove truly acceptable, it must first be Americanized as it were, that is to say, penetrated by the new-world conscience and cleansed of its taint of "evil." This tension between the impulse to plunge into "experience" and the impulse to renounce it is the chief source of the internal yet astonishingly abundant Jamesian emotion; and because the tension is not always adequately resolved, we sometimes get that effect, so well described by Glenway Wescott, of "embarrassed passion and hinted meaning in excess of the narrated facts; the psychic content is too great for its container of elegantly forged happenings; it all overflows and slops about and is magnificently wasted." On this side of James we touch upon his relationship to Hawthorne, whose characters, likewise tempted by "experience," are held back by the fear of sin. And Hawthorne's ancestral idea of sin survives in James, though in a secularized form. It has entered the sensibility and been translated into a revulsion, an exasperated feeling, almost morbid in its sensitiveness, against any conceivable crudity of

84

scene or crudity of conduct. (The trouble with American life, he wrote, is not that it is "ugly"—the ugly can be strange and grotesque—but that it is "plain"; "even nature, in the western world, has the peculiarity of seeming rather crude and immature.") Any failure of discrimination is sin, whereas virtue is a compound of intelligence, moral delicacy and the sense of the past.

And Hawthorne's remembrance of the religious mythology of New England and his fanciful concern with it is replaced in James—and this too is a kind of transmutation—by the remembrance and fanciful concern with history. It was for the sake of Europe's historical "opulence" that he left his native land. Yet this idea is also managed by him in a contradictory fashion, and for this reason W. C. Brownell was able to say that he showed no real interest in the "course of history." Now as a critic Brownell had no eye for James's historical picture of the American experience in Europe; but it is true that on the whole James's sense of history is restricted by the point of view of the "passionate pilgrim" who comes to rest in the shade of civilization. Above all, he comes to enrich his personality. Thus there is produced the Jamesian conception of history as a static yet irreproachable standard, a beautiful display, a treasured background, whose function is at once to adorn and lend perspective to his well nigh metaphysical probing of personal relations, of the private life. There never was a writer so immersed in personal relations, and his consistency in this respect implies an antihistorical attitude. This helps to explain the peculiarities of his consciousness, which is intellectual yet at the same time indifferent to general ideas, deeply comprehensive yet unattached to any open philosophical motive.

These contradictions in James—and there are others besides those I have mentioned—are chiefly to be accounted for in terms of his situation as an American writer who experienced his nationality and the social class to which he belonged at once as an ordeal and as an inspiration. The "great world" is corrupt, yet it represents an irresistible goal. Innocence points to all the wanted things one has been deprived of, yet it is profound in its good faith and not to be tampered with without loss. History and culture are the supreme ideal, but why not make of them a strictly private possession? Europe is romance and reality and civilization, but the spirit resides in America. James never faltered in the maze of these contraries; he knew how to take hold of them creatively and weave them into the web of his art. And the secret of their combination is the secret of his irony and of his humor.

TOLSTOY: THE GREEN TWIG
AND THE BLACK TRUNK

The critic's euphoria in the Tolstoyan weather. Tolstoy and literature. The green twig and the black trunk. The art of Tolstoy is of such irresistible simplicity and truth, is at once so intense and so transparent in all of its effects, that the need is seldom felt to analyze the means by which it becomes what it is, that is to say, its method or sum of techniques. In the bracing Tolstoyan air, the critic, however addicted to analysis, cannot help doubting his own task, sensing that there is something presumptuous and even unnatural, which requires an almost artificial deliberateness of intention, in the attempt to dissect an art so wonderfully integrated that, coming under its sway, we grasp it as a whole long before we are able to summon sufficient consciousness to examine the arrangement and interaction of its component parts.

Tolstoy is the exact opposite of those writers, typical of the modern age, whose works are to be understood only in terms of their creative strategies and design. The most self-observant of men, whose books are scarcely conceivable apart from the ceaseless introspection of which they are the embodiment, Tolstoy was the least self-conscious in his use of the literary medium. That is chiefly because in him the cleavage between art and life is of a minimal nature. In a Tolstoyan novel it is never the division but always the unity of art and life which makes for illumination. This novel, bristling with significant choices and crucial acts, teeming with dramatic motives, is not articulated through a plot as we commonly know it in fiction; one might say that in a sense there are no plots in Tolstoy but simply the unquestioned and unalterable process of life itself; such is the astonishing immediacy with which he possesses his characters that he can dispense with manipulative techniques, as he dispenses with the belletristic devices of exaggeration, distortion, and dissimulation. The fable, that specifically literary contrivance, or anything else which is merely invented or made up to suit the occasion, is very rarely found in his work. Nor is style an element of composition of which he is especially aware; he has no interest in language as such; he is the enemy of rhetoric and every kind of artifice and virtuosity. The conception of writing as of something calculated and constructed—a conception, first formulated explicitly in startlingly modern terms by Edgar Allan Poe, upon which literary culture has become more and more dependent—is entirely foreign to Tolstoy.

All that is of a piece, of course, with his unique attitude toward literature, unique, that is, for a writer of modern times. For Tolstoy continually dissociated himself from literature whether considered matter-of-factly, as a profession like any other, or ideally as an autonomous way of life, a complete fate in the sense in which the French writers of Flaubert's generation conceived of it. In his youth a soldier who saw war at first hand, the proprietor and manager of Yasnaya Polyana, a husband and father not as other men are husbands and fathers but in what might be described as programmatic and even militant fashion, and subsequently a religious philosopher and the head of a sect, he was a writer through all the years—a writer, but never a litterateur, the very idea repelled him. The litterateur performs a function imposed by the social division of labor, and inevitably he pays the price of his

88

specialization by accepting and even applauding his own one-sidedness and conceit, his noncommitted state as witness and observer, and the necessity under which he labors of preying upon life for the themes that it yields. It is with pride that Tolstoy exempted Lermontov and himself from the class of "men of letters" while commiserating with Turgenev and Goncharov for being so much of it; and in his *Reminiscences of Tolstoy* Gorky remarks that he spoke of literature but rarely and little, "as if it were something alien to him."

To account for that attitude by tracing it back to Tolstoy's aristocratic status, as if he disdained to identify himself with a plebeian profession, is to take much too simple a view of his personality. The point is, rather, that from the very first Tolstoy instinctively recognized the essential insufficiency and makeshift character of the narrowly aesthetic outlook, of the purely artistic appropriation of the world. His personality was built on too broad a frame to fit into an aesthetic mold, and he denied that art was anything more than the ornament and charm of life. He came of age at a time when the social group to which he belonged had not yet been thoroughly exposed to the ravages of the division of labor, when men of his stamp could still resist the dubious consolations it brings in its train. Endowed with enormous energies, possessed of boundless egoism and of an equally boundless power of conscience, he was capable, in Leo Shestov's phrase, of destroying and creating worlds, and before he was quite twenty-seven years old he had the audacity to declare his ambition, writing it all solemnly down in his diary, of becoming the founder of "a new religion corresponding with the present state of mankind; the religion of Christ but purged of dogmas and mysticism—a practical religion, not promising future bliss but giving bliss on earth." No wonder, then, that while approaching the task of mastering the literary medium with the utmost seriousness, and prizing that mastery as a beautiful accomplishment, he could not but dismiss the pieties of art as trivial compared with the question he faced from the very beginning, the question he so heroically sought to answer even in his most elemental creations, in which he seems to us to move through the natural world with splendid and miraculous ease, more fully at home there than any other literary artist. Yet even in those creations the very same question appears now in a manifest and now in a latent fashion, always the same question: How to live, what to do?

In 1880, when Turgenev visited Yasnaya Polyana after a long estrangement, he wrote a letter bewailing Tolstoy's apparent desertion of art. "I, for instance, am considered an artist," he said, "but what am I compared with him? In contemporary European literature he has no equal. . . . But what is one to do with him. He has plunged headlong into another sphere: he has surrounded himself with Bibles and Gospels in all languages, and has written a whole heap of papers. He has a trunk full of these mystical ethics and of various pseudo-interpretations. He read me some of it, which I simply do not understand. . . . I told him, 'That is not the real thing'; but he replied: 'It is just the real thing'. . . . Very probably he will give nothing more to literature, or if he reappears it will be with that trunk." Turgenev was wrong. Tolstoy gave a great deal more to literature, and it is out of that same trunk, so offensive in the eyes of the accomplished man of letters, that he brought forth such masterpieces as *The Death of Ivan Ilyich* and *Master and Man*, plays like *The Power of Darkness*, also many popular tales which, stripped of all ornament, have an essential force and grace of their own, and together with much that is abstract and overrationalized, not a few expository works, like *What Then Must We Do?*, which belong with the most powerful revolutionary writings of the modern age. For it is not for nothing that Tolstoy was always rummaging in that black trunk. At the bottom of it, underneath a heap of old papers, there lay a little *mana*-object, a little green twig which he carried with him through the years, a twig of

90

which he was told at the age of five by his brother Nicholas—that it was buried by the road at the edge of a certain ravine and that on it was inscribed the secret by means of which "all men would cease suffering misfortunes, leave off quarreling and being angry, and become continuously happy." The legend of the green twig was part of a game played by the Tolstoy children, called the Ant-Brothers, which consisted of crawling under chairs screened off by shawls and cuddling together in the dark. Tolstoy asked to be buried on the very spot at the edge of the ravine at Yasnaya Polyana which he loved because of its association with the imaginary green twig and the ideal of human brotherhood. And when he was an old man he wrote that "the idea of ant-brothers lovingly clinging to one another, though not under two arm-chairs curtained by shawls but of all mankind under the wide dome of heaven, has remained unaltered in me. As I then believed that there existed a little green twig whereon was written the message which would destroy all evil in men and give them universal welfare, so I now believe that such truth exists and will be revealed to men and will give them all it promises." It is clear that the change in Tolstoy by which Turgenev was so appalled was entirely natural, was presupposed by all the conditions of his development and of his creative consciousness. In the total Tolstoyan perspective the black trunk of his old age represents exactly the same thing as the green twig of his childhood.

Even the crude heresies he expounded in *What is Art?* lose much of their offensiveness in that perspective. In itself when examined without reference to the author's compelling grasp of the central and most fearful problems of human existence, the argument of that book strikes us as a willful inflation of the idea of moral utility at the expense of the values of the imagination. But actually the fault of the argument is not that it is wholly implausible —as a matter of fact, it is of long and reputable lineage in the history of culture—as that it is advanced recklessly and with a logic at once narrow and excessive; the Tolstoyan insight is here vitiated in the same way as the insight into sexual relations is vitiated in *The Kreutzer Sonata*. Still, both works, the onslaught on modern love and marriage as well as the onslaught on the fetishism of art to which the modern sensibility has succumbed, are significantly expressive of Tolstoy's spiritual crisis—a crisis badly understood by many people, who take it as a phenomenon disruptive of his creative power despite the fact that, in the last analysis, it is impossible to speak of two Tolstoys, the creative and the noncreative, for there is no real discontinuity in his career. Though there is a contradiction between the artist and the moralist in him, his personality retains its basic unity, transcending all contradictions. Boris Eichenbaum, one of the very best of Tolstoy's Russian critics, has observed that the spiritual crisis did not operate to disrupt his art because it was a crisis internally not externally determined, the prerequisite of a new act of cognition through which he sought to re-arm his genius and to ascertain the possibility of new creative beginnings. Thus *My Confession*, with which Tolstoy's later period opens and which appeared immediately after *Anna Karenina*, is unmistakably a work of the imagination and at the same time a mighty feat of consciousness.

Six years after writing *What is Art?* Tolstoy finished *Hadji Murad* (1904), one of the finest nouvelles in the Russian language and a model of narrative skill and objective artistry. Is not the song of the nightingales, that song of life and death which bursts into ecstasy at dawn on the day when Hadji Murad attempts to regain his freedom, the very same song which rises in that marvelously sensual scene in *Family Happiness*, a scene bathed in sunlight, when Masha, surprising Sergey Mikhaylych in the cherry orchard, enjoys for the first time the full savor of her youthful love? *Hadji Murad* was written not less than forty-five years after *Family Happiness*. And in *The Devil*—a moral tale, the product, like *The Kreutzer Sonata*, of Tolstoy's most sectarian period and extremest assertion of dogmatic ascetism—what we remember best is not Eugene Irtenev's torments of conscience, his efforts to subdue his passion, but precisely the description of his carnal meetings in the sundrenched woods with Stepanida, the fresh and strong peasant-girl with full breasts and bright black eyes. The truth is that in the struggle between the old moralist and the old magician in Tolstoy both gave as good as they got.

The rationalist and anti-Romantic in Tolstoy. Sources in the eighteenth century. Divergence from the intelligentsia. Creative method. Tolstoy has been described as the least neurotic of all the great Russians, and by the same token he can be said to be more committed than any of them to the rational understanding and ordering of life and to the throwing off of romantic illusions. Unlike Dostoevsky, he owes nothing either to the so-called natural school of Gogol or to the Romantic movement in western literature. The school of Gogol is a school of morbidity, whereas Tolstoy is above all an artist of the normal—the normal, however, so intensified that it acquires a poetical truth and an emotional fullness which we are astounded to discover in the ordinary situations of life. Analysis is always at the center of the Tolstoyan creation. It is the sort of analysis, however, which has little in common with the analytical modes of such novelists as Dostoevsky and Proust, for example, both characteristically modern though in entirely different ways. While in their work analysis is precipitated mainly by deviations from the norm, from the broad standard of human conduct, in Tolstoy the analysis remains in line with that standard, is in fact inconceivable apart from it. Dostoevsky's "underground" man, who is a bundle of plebeian resentments, is unimaginable in a Tolstoyan novel. Even in Tolstoy's treatment of death there is nothing actually morbid—certainly not in the description of the death of Prince Andrey in *War and Peace* and of Nikolay Levin in *Anna Karenina*. As for *The Death of Ivan Ilyich*, that story

93

would be utterly pointless if we were to see Ivan Ilyich as a special type and what happened to him as anything out of the ordinary. Ivan Ilyich is Everyman, and the state of absolute solitude into which he falls as his life ebbs away is the existential norm, the inescapable realization of mortality. Nothing could be more mistaken than the idea that Tolstoy's concern with death is an abnormal trait. On the contrary, if anything it is a supernormal trait, for the intensity of his concern with death is proportionate to the intensity of his concern with life. Of Tolstoy it can be said that he truly lived his life, and for that very reason he was so tormented by the thought of dying. It was a literal thought, physical through and through, a vital manifestation of the simplicity with which he grasped man's life in the world. This simplicity is of a metaphysical nature, and in it, as one Russian critic has remarked, you find the essence of Tolstoy's world-view, the energizing and generalizing formula that served him as the means unifying the diverse motives of his intellectual and literary experience. It is due to this metaphysical simplicity that he was unable to come to terms with any system of dogmatic theology and that in the end, despite all his efforts to retain it, he was compelled to exclude even the idea of God from his own system of rationalized religion. Thus all notions of immortality seemed absurd to Tolstoy, and his scheme of salvation was entirely calculated to make men happy here and now. It is reported of Thoreau that when he lay dying his answer to all talk of the hereafter was "one world at a time." That is the sort of answer with which Tolstoy's mentality is wholly in accord.

The way in which his rationalism enters his art is shown in his analysis of character, an analysis which leaves nothing undefined, nothing unexplained. That systematization of ambiguity which marks the modern novel is organically alien to Tolstoy. Given the framework in which his characters move we are told everything that we need to know or want to know about them. The tangled intimate life, the underside of their consciousness, their author is not

94

concerned with: he sets them up in the known world and sees them through their predicaments, however irksome and baffling, without ever depriving them of the rationality which supports their existence. For just as in Tolstoy's religiosity there is no element of mysticism, so in his creative art there is no element of mystery.

Unlike most of his contemporaries, Tolstoy did not pass through the school of Romanticism, and perhaps that is the reason he never hesitated to strike out the dark areas in the space in which he outlined his leading figures. He has few links with the literary culture evolved in Russia after 1820; the fact is that he has more in common with his literary grandfathers than with his literary fathers. Insofar as he has any literary affiliations at all they go back to the eighteenth century, to Rousseau, to Sterne, to the French classical drama, and in Russia to the period of Karamzin, Zhukovsky, Novikov, and Radichev. He has their robustness and skepticism. His quarrels with Turgenev, his inability to get on with the liberal and radical writers grouped around the *Contemporary*, a Petersburg periodical edited by the poet Nekrasov in which Tolstoy's first stories were published, are explained not so much by personal factors, such as his intractability of temper, as by the extreme differences between the conditions of his development and those of the Russian intelligentsia, whose rise coincides with the appearance of the plebeian on the literary scene. Tolstoy's family background was archaistic, not in the sense of provincial backwardness, but in the sense of the deliberate and even stylized attempt made by his family—more particularly his father—to preserve at Yasnaya Polyana the patriarchal traditions of the Russian nobility of the eighteenth century. It was a conscious and militant archaism directed against the "new" civilization of Petersburg, with its state-bureaucracy and merchant princes. The young Tolstoy was scornful of the "theories" and "convictions" held by the writers he met in Petersburg in the 1850's; instead of putting his trust in "theories" and "convictions" he relied on those Franklinesque rules and precepts of conduct with which he filled his diaries—rules and precepts he deduced from his idea of unalterable "moral instincts." In Nekrasov's circle he was regarded as a "wild man," a "troglodyte"; and in the early 1860's, when he set out on his second European tour, Nekrasov and his friends hoped that he would return in a mood of agreement with their notions of education and historical progress. Nothing came of it, of course, for he returned armed with more of those "simplifications" that cut under their assumptions. But if the Westernizers found no comfort in Tolstoy, neither did the Slavophils. The latters' ideology, with its forced and artificial doctrine of superiority to the West, was also aligned with plebeian social tasks; at bottom it represented the discomfiture of a small and weak plebeian class in a semifeudal society, a discomfiture idealized through national messianism. It was an obscurantist ideology incompatible with Tolstoy's belief in self-improvement and in the possibility of human perfection. Moreover, in Tolstoy's approach to western culture there was no distress, no anger, no hostility. He was never put off by it, for he considered European culture to be a natural sphere the products of which he could appropriate at will, and in any order he pleased, without in the least committing himself to its inner logic. He felt no more committed by his use of western ideas than the French-speaking gentry in *War and Peace* feel obligated to import the social institutions of France along with its language. Thus Tolstoy was able to sort out western tendencies to suit himself, as in *War and Peace,* where he is to some extent indebted for his conception of Napoleon to certain French publicists of the 1850's and 60's, who in their endeavor to deflate the pretensions of Napoleon III went so far in their polemics as also to blot out the image of his illustrious ancestor. Again, in that novel he is partly indebted for his so-called organic idea of war to Proudhon's book *La Guerre et la Paix,* which came out in a Russian translation in

1864. (Tolstoy had met Proudhon in Brussels in March, 1861.) And the arbitrary way in which he helped himself to the ideas of western thinkers is shown by the fact that he entirely ignored Proudhon's enthusiastic affirmation of Napoleon's historical role. The West was the realm of the city, a realm so strange to Tolstoy that he could regard it as neutral territory. The city was essentially unreal to him; he believed in the existence solely of the landowners and of the peasants. The contrast between Dostoevsky and Tolstoy, which Merezhkovsky and after him Thomas Mann have presented in terms of the abstract typology of the "man of spirit" as against the "man of nature," is more relevantly analyzed in terms of the contradiction between city and country, between the alienated intellectual proletariat of the city and the unalienated patriciate-peasantry of the country.

Much has been written concerning the influence of Rousseau on Tolstoy, but here again it is necessary to keep in mind that in western literature we perceive the Rousseauist ideas through the colored screen of Romanticism while in Tolstoy Rousseau survives through his rationalism no less than through his sensibility. In point of fact, the Rousseauist cult of nature is operative in Tolstoy in a manner that leads toward realism, as is seen in his Caucasian tales, for instance. If these tales now seem romantic to us, it is largely because of the picturesque material of which they are composed. A narrative like *The Cossacks* is actually turned in a tendencious way against the tradition of "caucasian romanticism" in Russian literature—the tradition of Pushkin, Lermontov, and Marlinsky. Olenin, the protagonist of *The Cossacks,* is so little of a Romantic hero that he is incapable of dominating even his own story; the impression of his personality is dissipated as the attention shifts to the Cossack lad Lukashka, to Daddy Eroshka, and to the girl Marianka. Think what Chateaubriand would have made of a heroine like Marianka. In Tolstoy, however, she is portrayed in an authentically natural style, with all the calm strength, unawareness of subjective values, and indifference of a primitive human being. Though she is a "child of nature" and therefore an object of poetical associations, she is seen much too soberly to arouse those high-flown sentiments which "nature" inspires in Romantic poets like Novalis or even the Goethe of *Werther*. Where the Romantics convert nature into a solace for the trials of civilization, into a theater of lyrical idleness and noble pleasures, Tolstoy identifies nature with work, independence, self-possession.

Compared with Pierre, Prince Andrey, or Levin, Olenin is a weak hero, but he is important in that in his reflections he sums up everything which went into the making of the early Tolstoy and which was in later years given a religious twist and offered as a doctrine of world-salvation. The primacy which the issue of happiness assumes in Olenin's thoughts is the key to his Tolstoyan nature. "Happiness is this," he said to himself, "happiness lies in living for others. That is evident. The desire for happiness is innate in every man; therefore it is legitimate. When trying to satisfy it selfishly—that is, by seeking for oneself riches, fame, comforts, or love—it may happen that circumstances arise which make it impossible to satisfy these desires. It follows that it is these desires which are illegitimate, but not the need for happiness. But what desires can always be satisfied despite external circumstances? What are they? Love, self-sacrifice." In these few sentences we get the quintessence of the Tolstoyan mentality: the belief that ultimate truth can be arrived at through common-sense reasoning, the utilitarian justification of the values of love and self-sacrifice and their release from all otherworldly sanctions, the striving for the simplification of existence which takes the form of a return to a life closer to nature—a return, however, involving a self-consciousness and a constant recourse to reason that augurs ill for the success of any such experiment.

Tolstoy's art is so frequently spoken of as "organic" that one is likely to overlook the rationalistic structure on which it is based. This structure consists of successive layers of concrete details, physical and psychological, driven into place and held together by a generalization or dogma. Thus in *The Cossacks* the generalization is the idea of the return to nature; in *Two Hussars* it is the superiority of the older Turbin to the younger, that is to say, of the more naive times of the past to the "modern" period. (The original title of the story was *Father and Son*.) The binding dogma in *Family Happiness* is the instability and deceptiveness of love as compared with a sound family life and the rearing of children in insuring the happiness of a married couple. Yet the didacticism of such ideas seldom interferes with our enjoyment of the Tolstoyan fiction. For the wonderful thing about it is its tissue of detail, the tenacious way in which it holds together, as if it were a glutinous substance, and its incomparable rightness and truthfulness.

Parallelism of construction is another leading characteristic of the Tolstoyan method. In *War and Peace,* in the chronicle of the lives of the Bolkonsky and Rostov families, this parallelism is not devised dramatically, as a deliberate contrast, but in other narratives it is driven toward a stark comparison, as between Anna and Vronsky on the one hand and Kitty and Levin on the other in *Anna Karenina,* or between two generations in *Two Hussars,* or between Lukashka and Olenin in *The Cossacks*. One writer on Tolstoy put it very well when he said that in the Tolstoyan novel all ideas and phenomena exist in pairs. Comparison is inherent in his method.

His early *nouvelles* can certainly be read and appreciated without reference to their historical context, to the ideological differences between him and his contemporaries which set him off to confound them with more proofs of his disdain for their "progressive" opinions. Still, the origin of *Family Happiness* in the quarrels of the period is worth recalling. At that time (in the 1850's) public opinion was much exercised over the question of free love and the emancipation of women; George Sand was a novelist widely read in intellectual circles, and of course most advanced people agreed with George Sand's libertarian solution of the question. Not so Tolstoy, who opposed all such tendencies, for he regarded marriage and family life as the foundations of society. Thus *Family Happiness,* with its denigration of love and of equal rights for women, was conceived, quite apart from its personal genesis in Tolstoy's affair with Valerya Arsenev, as a polemical rejoinder to George Sand, then adored by virtually all the Petersburg writers, including Dostoevsky.

The faith in family life is integral of Tolstoy. It has the deepest psychological roots in his private history, and socially it exemplifies his championship of patriarchal relations. It is a necessary part of his archaistic outlook, which in later life was transformed into a special kind of radicalism, genuinely revolutionary in some of its aspects and thoroughly archaistic in others. *War and Peace* is as much a chronicle of certain families as an historical novel. The historical sense is not really native to Tolstoy. His interest in the period of 1812 is peculiarly his own, derived from his interest in the story of his own family. He began work on *Anna Karenina* after failing in the attempt to write another historical novel, a sequel to *War and Peace.* And *Anna Karenina* is of course the novel in which his inordinate concern with marriage and family life receives its fullest expression.

The existential center of the Tolstoyan art. Tolstoy as the last of the unalienated artists. So much has been made here of the rationalism of Tolstoy that it becomes necessary to explain how his art is saved from the ill effects of it. Art and reason are not naturally congruous with one another, and many a work of the imagination has miscarried because of an excess of logic. "There may be a system of logic; a system of being there can never be," said Kierkegaard. And art is above all a recreation of individual being; the system-maker must perforce abstract from the real world while the artist, if he is true to his medium, recoils from the process of abstraction because it

100

is precisely the irreducible quality of life, its multiple divulgements in all their uniqueness and singularity, which provoke his imagination.

Now there is only one novel of Tolstoy's that might be described as a casualty of his rationalism, and that is *Resurrection*. The greater part of his fiction is existentially centered in a concrete inwardness and subjectivity by which it gains its quality of genius. In this sense it becomes possible to say that Tolstoy is much more a novelist of life and death than he is of good and evil—good and evil are not categories of existence but of moral analysis. And the binding dogmas or ideas of Tolstoy's fiction are not in contradiction with its existential sense; on the contrary, their interaction is a triumph of creative tact and proof of the essential wholeness of Tolstoy's nature. The Tolstoyan characters grasp their lives through their total personalities, not merely through their intellects. Their experience is full of moments of shock, of radical choice and decision, when they confront themselves in the terrible and inevitable aloneness of their being. To mention but one of innumerable instances of such spiritual confrontation, there is the moment in *Anna Karenina* when Anna's husband begins to suspect her relation to Vronsky. That is the moment when the accepted and taken-for-granted falls to pieces, when the carefully built-up credibility of the world is torn apart by a revelation of its underlying irrationality. For according to Alexey Alexandrovitch's ideas one ought to have confidence in one's wife because jealousy was insulting to oneself as well as to her. He had never really asked himself why his wife deserved such confidence and why he believed that she would always love him. But now, though he still felt that jealousy was a bad and shameful state, "he also felt that he was standing face to face with something illogical and irrational, and did not know what was to be done. Alexey Alexandrovitch was standing face to face with life, with the possibility of his wife's loving some one other than himself, and this seemed to him very irrational and incomprehensible because it was life itself. All his life Alexey Alexandrovitch had lived and worked in official spheres, having to do with the reflection of life. And every time he stumbled against life itself he had shrunk away from it. Now he experienced a feeling akin to that of a man who, while calmly crossing a precipice by a bridge, should suddenly discover that the bridge is broken, and that there is a chasm below. That chasm was life itself, the bridge that artificial life in which Alexey Alexandrovitch had lived. For the first time the question presented itself to him of the possibility of his wife's loving some one else, and he was horrified at it."

It is exactly this "standing face to face with life," and the realization that there are things in it that are irreducible and incomprehensible, which drew Tolstoy toward the theme of death. Again and again he returned to this theme, out of a fear of death which is really the highest form of courage. Most people put death out of their minds because they cannot bear to think of it. Gorky reports that Tolstoy once said to him that "if a man has learned to think, no matter what he may think about, he is always thinking of his own death. All philosophers were like that. And what truths can there be, if there is death?" That is a statement of despair and nihilism the paradox of which is that it springs from the depths of Tolstoy's existential feeling of life; and this is because the despair and nihilism spring not from the renunciation but from the affirmation of life; Tolstoy never gave up the search for an all-embracing truth, for a rational justification of man's existence on the earth.

The fact is that Tolstoy was at bottom so sure in his mastery of life and so firm in his inner feeling of security that he could afford to deal intimately with death. Consider the difference in this respect between him and Franz Kafka, another novelist of the existential mode. In Kafka the theme of death is absent, not because of strength but rather because of neurotic weakness. He was ridden by a conviction, as he himself defined it, of "complete helplessness," and baffled by the seeming impossibility of solving even the most elementary problems of living, he could not look beyond life into the face of death. He wrote: "Without ancestors, without marriage, without progeny, with an unbridled desire for ancestors, marriage, and progeny. All stretch out their hands towards me: ancestors, marriage, and progeny, but from a point far too remote from me." That is the complaint of an utterly alienated man, without a past and without a future. Tolstoy, on the other hand, was attached with the strongest bonds to the patrician-peasant life of Yasnaya Polyana, he was in possession of the world and of his own humanity. His secret is that he is the last of the unalienated artists. Hence it is necessary to insist on the differences not so much between him and other artists generally as between him and the modern breed of alienated artists. It is thanks to this unalienated condition that he is capable of moving us powerfully when describing the simplest, the most ordinary and therefore in their own way also the gravest occasions of life—occasions that the alienated artist can approach only from a distance, through flat naturalistic techniques, or through immense subtleties of analysis, or through the transposition of his subject onto the plane of myth and fantasy.

But, of course, even Tolstoy, being a man of the nineteenth century, could not finally escape the blight of alienation. In his lifetime Russian society disintegrated; he witnessed the passing of the old society of status and its replacement by a cruelly impersonal system of bourgeois relations. Tolstoy resisted the catastrophic ruin of the traditional order by straining all the powers of his reason to discover a way out. His so-called conversion is the most dramatic and desperate episode in his stubborn and protracted struggle against alienation. His attack on civilization is essentially an attack on the conditions that make for alienation. The doctrine of Christian anarchism, developed after his conversion, reflects, as Lenin put it, "the accumulated hate, the ripened aspiration for a better

103

life, the desire to throw off the past—and also the immaturity, the dreamy contemplativeness, the political inexperience, and the revolutionary flabbiness of the villages." Still, the point of that doctrine lies not in its religious content, which is very small indeed, but rather in its formulation of a social ideal and of a utopian social program.

AN INTRODUCTION TO KAFKA*

Franz Kafka is today firmly linked in the literary mind to such names as Joyce and Proust and Yeats and Rilke and Eliot—the sacred untouchables, as they have been rightly called, of the modern creative line. Among them he is exceptional in that he enjoyed no public recognition of consequence in his lifetime, for he withheld his longer narratives from publication and was scarcely known beyond a narrow circle of German writers. His posthumous world-fame came to him only in the past two decades.

The first translation of one of his books appeared in this country in 1930, six years after his death. That book was *The Castle,* a novel that ranks high in the Kafka canon. Few readers were then able to gauge its true worth, and even as late as 1937, when *The Trial* was brought out here, it was chiefly Kafka's apparent mystifications rather than his pattern of meaning and basic motives that aroused interest. Readers were astonished by his work but hardly convinced of its importance. Since then his idiosyncratic but powerful sensibility has entered into the blood stream of twentieth-century literature. He has been made the subject of numerous critical studies in

---

* Written as an introduction to the *Selected Tales of Franz Kafka* in the Modern Library edition (1952).

many languages; and everywhere the more sensitive younger writers, conscious of the static condition of the prevailing fictional techniques and seeking creative renewal, have taken his example to heart. There can be little doubt any longer of his stature as an artist in the metaphysical mode, whose concern is with the ultimate structure of human existence, or of his surpassing originality as an innovator in creative method. Like Rilke in the *Duino Elegies* he asked the supreme question: *Was war wirklich im All?* (What was real in the world?)

A master of narrative tone, of a subtle, judicious and ironically conservative style, Kafka combines in his fiction the real and the unreal, extreme subjectivity of content with forms rigorously objective, a lovingly exact portrayal of the factual world with dreamlike dissolution of it. By unifying these contrary elements he was able to achieve a fundamentally new appropriation of the resources of the prose medium. This much can be said, I think, without attempting to give an integrated critical estimate of his work, which may well be premature even now. The analysis and description of its qualities will suffice. Thus it is clear that if Kafka so compellingly arouses in us a sense of immediate relatedness, of strong even if uneasy identification, it is because of the profound quality of his feeling for the experience of human loss, estrangement, guilt, and anxiety—an experience increasingly dominant in the modern age.

That Kafka is among the most neurotic of literary artists goes without saying. It accounts, mainly, for the felt menace of his fantastic symbolism and for his drastic departure from the well-defined norms of the literary imagination. For all its obviousness, however, the fact of Kafka's neuroticism presents a danger, if not a vulgar tempation, to the unliterary mind, which tends to confuse a fact so patent with critical judgment and appraisal. No greater error is possible in our approach to literary art. To avoid that common error it is above all necessary to perceive that Kafka is something more than a neurotic artist; he is also an artist of neurosis, that is to say, he succeds in objectifying through imaginative means the states of mind typical of neurosis and hence in incorporating his private world into the public world we all live in. Once that is accomplished, the creative writer has performed the essential operation which is the secret of his triumph as an artist, if not as a man; he has exorcised his demon, freed himself of his personal burden, converting us into his accomplices. And we, as good readers, as willing accomplices, have no real reason to complain. Neurosis may be the occasion but literature is the consequence. Moreover, the creative writer is the last person we may look to if our concern is with drawing a line between the normal and the abnormal. For whatever the practicing psychologist may make of that crude though useful distinction, the artist cannot attend to it without inhibiting his sense of life in its full concreteness and complexity.

The novelist Graham Greene has remarked that "every creative writer worth our consideration, every writer who can be called in the wide sense of the term a poet, is a victim: a man given over to an obsession." Kafka's obsession was an inordinate sense of inadequacy, failure and sinfulness—a sinfulness corresponding to nothing he had actually done or left undone, but lodged in the innermost recesses of his being. "The state in which we find ourselves is sinful, quite independently of guilt," he wrote in his notebook. The clue to *The Trial* is the reflection that "only our concept of time makes it possible for us to speak of the Day of Judgment by that name; in reality it is a summary court in perpetual session." And in the same sequence of reflections we find the perfectly typical sentence: "The hunting dogs are playing in the courtyard, but the hare will not escape them, no matter how fast it may be flying already through the woods." The identification here is plainly with the hare; and with the hunting dogs, too, insofar as they represent the hare's longing for self-punishment, his inner wish to be cornered, to be hurt and torn to pieces so as to atone for the guilt that fills him from

107

top to bottom. In this one short sentence about the hare and the dogs you have the gist of the typical Kafkan narrative, the obsessive theme, the nuclear fable concerning the victim of an unappeasable power to which he returns again and again, varying and complicating its structure with astonishing resourcefulness, and erecting on so slender a foundation such marvelous superstructures as that of the myth of the Old Commander in "In the Penal Colony," the myth of the Law in *The Trial,* and of the celestial bureaucracy in *The Castle.*

The simplicity of the nuclear fable in Kafka should not lead us, however, to disregard the qualities that make him one of the most enigmatic figures in world literature. It does no good to speak of him as an author of religious allegories. Unlike such religious allegorists as Dante or Bunyan he does not depend on the definitive logic of a generally known system of theology; his creative mode presupposes no body of knowledge external to itself; he is not allegorical in any accepted sense but rather an innovator so deeply individualistic as to fit none of the familiar categories. Also, the difficulty of understanding him is on a different plane from that encountered in reading a novelist like James Joyce, for example. Whereas the obscurities of the latter are inherent in the elaborate stylization of his material and in his complex structural designs, in Kafka's case it is the meaning alone that baffles us. Both in language and construction he is elementary compared to Joyce, yet many readers have been mystified by his fictions. But the mystification is gradually cleared up once we learn to listen attentively to his tone and become accustomed to the complete freedom with which he suspends certain conventions of storytelling when it suits his symbolic purpose. Thus when we read in the first sentence of "The Metamorphosis" that the clerk Gregor Samsa awoke one morning to find himself changed into a gigantic insect, it is a mistake to think that by means of this bold stroke Kafka intends to call into question the laws of nature. What he calls into question, rather, is
108

the convention that the laws of nature are at all times to be observed in fiction; and having suspended that convention in the very first paragraph of the story, from that point on he develops it in a logical and realistic manner. The clerk's metamorphosis is a multiple symbol of his alienation from the human state, of his "awakening" to the full horror of his dull, spiritless existence, and of the desperate self-disgust of his unconscious fantasy-life, in which the wish to displace the father and take over his authority in the family is annulled by the guilt-need to suffer a revolting punishment for his presumption.

Another type of symbolism, far less psychologically charged, is found in stories like "The Great Wall of China." What is the Great Wall? It is likewise a multiple symbol—of human solidarity, of earthly fulfillment and of mankind's effort to obtain supernatural guidance. But why was the wall built in a piecemeal fashion, thus permitting the nomads of the North to slip through the gaps? The reply is that it is in the nature of man to achieve only limited ends. He cannot comprehend the Whole; his vision is discontinuous, his security always incomplete; his aims he can realize only in fragmentary fashion. No doubt the "high command" is ultimately responsible for the apparently inexpedient method of the wall's construction; yet it would never do to question its decrees. Not that such questioning is blasphemous in itself but rather that in the long run it is useless. Logic can bring us only to a certain point. Beyond that an answer of a sort is given by the beautiful parable of the river in spring. And as the story continues, the theme of the wall is dialectically converted into a series of poetic speculations concerning the relationship between the Chinese and the imperial court at Pekin, that is between God and man. While in "Investigations of a Dog" the remoteness of God is represented as a remoteness in time, in this story the imagery is chiefly spatial. Pekin is so far away from the villagers of the South that they can hardly imagine its existence. They worship dynasties long

109

since dead; news arriving from the imperial court is obsolete by the time it reaches them. This inability of the "Chinese" to possess their Emperor in his vital contemporaneity appears to be a reflection on the idea of God as known to modern man—an idea ill-defined, nebulous and, above all, archaic. Man is now unaware of the real powers that govern his life; insofar as he has any knowledge of divinity it is as of something purely historical.

The quarrel between the religious and the psychoanalytic interpreters of Kafka is of no great moment, as his work is sufficiently meaningful to support some of the "truths" of both schools. Thus the father who condemns his son to death by drowning (in "The Judgment") can be understood as the tyrannical father of Freudian lore and at the same time as the God of Judgment rising in His wrath to destroy man's illusion of self-sufficiency in the world. At bottom there is no conflict between the two interpretations. For one thing, they are not mutually exclusive; for another, the reading we give the story depends as much on our own outlook—within certain limits of course—as on that of the author. There was in Kafka's character an element of radical humility not permitting him to set out to "prove" any given attitude toward life or idea about it. This he plainly tells us in some of the aphorisms that he wrote about himself in the third person: "He proves nothing but himself, his sole proof is himself, all his opponents overcome him at once, not by refuting him (he is irrefutable) but by proving themselves."

That Kafka was a man of religious temper I have no doubt. Though the creator of a surpassing imagery of human failure and frustration, inclined to feel imprisoned on this earth, afflicted with "the melancholy, the impotence, the sicknesses, the feverish fancies of the captive," he never abandons his trust in the spirituality of existence, in the "indestructible," and is disheartened by his literary effort because he wants his writing to attain the power of lifting the world into the realm of "the pure,

110

the true, the immutable." Yet there is nothing either in his private papers or in his fiction to warrant the claim that he was a believer in a personal God who gave his assent to any of the dogmatic systems associated with institutional religion. Even original sin, the dogma closest to the thematic center of his work, he interprets speculatively as "consisting of the complaint, which man makes and never ceases making, that a wrong had been done to him, that the original sin was committed upon him." From the standpoint of the theologian that is sheer heresy, gentle, self-incriminating heresy, to be sure, but heresy nevertheless. The German critic Franz Blei, who was personally acquainted with Kafka, speaks of him as "the servant of a God not believed in." A piety so paradoxical, so immune to categorical definition, so removed from the fixed and traditional, refusing the consolation of revealed religion yet intent on winning through to "a faith like a guillotine, as heavy, as light," could never have found expression in general ideas or logical thought but only in the language of art, the one language capable of offering everything while claiming nothing, asserting nothing, proving nothing.

Born in 1883 of middle-class Jewish parents, Kafka appears to have lost his self-confidence early in life, exchanging for it, as he himself put it, "a boundless sense of guilt." Moods of loss and failure, and the idea of the insolubility even of the most ordinary human problems, depressed his youth and later inspired his art. In the center of his life stands the father, a figure fully corresponding to that Freudian terror, the Primal Sire. Energetic, overbearing, capricious, successful, respectable, the father, not so much by malicious intention as by being simply what he was, exposed to ridicule his son's impractical inclinations and spiritual wanderings. The mother, though solicitous for her son, was far too much absorbed in her husband to play an independent role; and young Franz was thus driven to extremes of loneliness and introspection that continually negated themselves in the idea of integra-

111

tion through marriage, children, and the practice of an honorable profession ("a true calling . . . the right vocation"). The effect on him of his father was such that though he usually talked exceedingly well, in the presence of the formidable parent he took to stuttering. "For me," he wrote to his father in later life, "you began to have that mysterious quality which all tyrants have, whose privilege is based on their personality, not on reason." It is clear that the source of the principle of authority so characteristic of his art is to be traced to his ambivalent attitude to his father, an attitude of strong repulsion as well as identification. Constructed out of elements of his own personality, the protagonist of his major fictions is coerced by extranatural powers who are continually justified and exalted even as they are made to manifest themselves in the guise of a menacing and arbitrary bureaucracy. Max Brod, Kafka's lifelong friend, biographer, and editor of his posthumous writings, relates that in many talks he attempted to demonstrate to him the foolishness of his self-contempt and chronic overestimation of his father. These talks were useless, for Kafka produced a "torrent of arguments" that shattered and repelled his friend, who soon realized that only from the standpoint of an outsider could it be asked: "What difference could his father's approval make to Kafka?" His need for that approval was obviously "an innate, irrefutable feeling" that lasted to the end of his life.

In 1906 he took his degree in law at the German University in Prague and soon afterwards obtained a post in an accident-insurance office. But his real interest was in writing, which he approached with the utmost moral earnestness, regarding it as a sacred expenditure of energy, an effort at communion with one's fellow-men, the reflected splendor of religious perception. However, it could never serve as his means of livelihood; aside from his objection in principle to turning literary talent into a source of material benefits, there were other obstacles. He wrote at a pace altogether his own, filled with a raging discontent; at the same time there was the drastic need to stand on his own feet, to win immediate independence from the family. Yet the work at the insurance office disintegrated him; the two occupations were incompatible.

In his letters he writes of literature as his only hope for happiness and fulfillment; and telling of trancelike states when he felt himself at the boundary of the human, he adds that they lacked the serenity of inspiration and were not conducive to the best writing. He speaks of himself as having been on the way to create "a new secret doctrine, a Kabala," but his replies as to the meaning of that doctrine are as diverse as they are contradictory. (His precision, Brod rightly says, was moral, not intellectual.) "I represent," we read in his diary, "the negative elements of my age. . . . Unlike Kierkegaard, I was not guided in life by the new heavily sinking hand of Christianity, nor have I caught hold, like the Zionists, of one of the ends of the flying prayer-shawl of the Jews." The one break in his relationship with Brod seems to have been caused by his coolness to Zionism. "What have I in common with the Jews," he wrote, "when I have scarcely anything in common with myself?" In later years, however, he developed a lively interest in the aspirations of the Zionists, studied Jewish folk-literature, the Hebrew language, and read the Talmud (to which his style, by the way, in its reasoning, argumentative quality, in its movement through assertion and contradiction, statement and refutation, bears some resemblance).

It was in 1912—a fateful year in his life—that he met Felice B., the young woman from Berlin whom he wanted to marry but was forced to renounce, suffering terrible anguish in twice breaking off his engagement to her. He felt that for a man in his uprooted condition, lacking independent status and a secure orientation in life, marriage was an impossible task. But that was the year, too, in which his literary intentions and continual probing of his own predicament came together in a way enabling him to forge decisively ahead in his work. Compared to what he wrote in the fall of that year everything he had previously written seems sketchy and unfinished. On the night of September 22 of that seminal fall he wrote "The Judgment" in one sitting, remarking afterwards that during that long stretch between ten o'clock in the evening and six o'clock the next morning he more than once carried his weight on his own back. "The Judgment" is the first Kafkan story which is all of a piece and the first in which the characteristic theme of the struggle between father and son is sounded to the depths. That same month and the next he wrote the long opening chapter of *Amerika,* his first novel, and in November he completed "The Metamorphosis," certainly his greatest story, in which he achieves an overpowering effect through his consummate handling of the factual detail that supports and actualizes the somber fantasy of the plot. This story is the very embodiment of that quality of the exigent and the extreme, that sense of a human being hemmed in by his own existence and absolutely committed to it, which touches us so deeply in Kafka because it is at once method and content, entreaty and response, the goal and the way. It is mainly through this "existential" quality that Kafka *substantiates* his world for us, imparting the unmistakable appeal of reality to those elements in it that might otherwise appear to be little more than the products of a bizarre or erratic imagination. In "The Metamorphosis," I would say, Kafka for the first time fully realized his own innermost conception of writing—a conception of inexpressible urgency and inwardness. Long before the composition of the story, he attempted to explain what writing meant to him when he said, in a letter to his friend Oskar Pollak, that "the books we need are of the kind that act upon us like a misfortune, that make us suffer like the death of someone we love more than ourselves, that make us feel as though we were on the verge of suicide, or lost in a forest remote from all human habitation—a book should serve as the ax for the frozen sea within us."

114

In October of that same year Max Brod notes in his diary: "Kafka in ecstasy. Writes all night long. . . ." And again: "Kafka in incredible ecstasy." There is something more to this ecstatic state than elation and the sense of freedom a writer normally experiences when making visible progress in his work. The patently compulsive nature of "The Judgment" and "The Metamorphosis," no less than Kafka's own comment upon them in his diaries, suggest that these stories served as "the ax for the frozen sea" within him—in other words, that the process of their creation involved a breakthrough to layers of repressed material which had heretofore proven inaccessible. It is as if in these psychodynamic fictions the neurotic sufferer in Kafka and the artist in him locked hands and held on for dear life. Precisely of works such as these one can say with Yeats that "the more unconscious the creation the more powerful."

The novel *Amerika,* begun in that period, stands somewhat apart from the bulk of Kafka's work. The extranatural plays no part in it; there is no evocation of mysterious powers or any derangement of the known and recognizable world for the sake of injecting into it the menace of the irrational and unfathomable. It is the only one of Kafka's longer narratives in which he fully indulged his flair for comedy. The intention behind it, however, is not the exposure of specific foibles but the portrayal of the typical human condition. "If sufficiently systematized comedy turns into reality," he wrote in his notebooks. And this statement can stand as the motto of this picaresque tale of the adventures of the sixteen-year-old boy Karl Rossmann, a native of Prague, in the mechanized cities of the United States, a country which Kafka had never seen but of which he had a definite image in his mind.

Steeped as he was in moods of loss and failure, he tended to regard with astonishment and inordinate admiration all examples of constructive will, of the ability of men to discover their true calling and achieve that integration in the community to which he attached the highest

115

value but which he believed to be beyond his own reach. His constant plaint was the same as that of the character in Hawthorne's story "The Intelligence Office," who never ceases to cry out: "I want my place, my own place, my proper sphere, my thing to do, which nature intended me to perform when she fashioned me thus awry, and which I have vainly sought all my lifetime!" For this reason Benjamin Franklin, who was singularly successful in all his undertakings, was among Kafka's favorite historical figures; and Franklin's *Autobiography* is one of the sources of *Amerika*. Let no one think, however, that Kafka was charmed by Poor Richard's opinion of himself or by his general philosophy; what interested him in this exemplary American career was its inexplicable element of fate, which in this case had manifested itself in a positive guise. He probably read Poor Richard's recommendations of virtue, his list of proverbs on frugality, temperance, moderation, tranquility, and the like, as one reads a work on strategy, interpreting those dismally sagacious sayings as so many moves in the complicated game of ingratiating oneself with the nameless authorities whose law, though its intent and meaning are unknown and unknowable, prevails none the less. It was the Ulysses-like aspect of Franklin that attracted Kafka, and he conceived of America as his Mediterranean. Americans, he thought, wore perpetual smiles on their faces, for somehow they had managed, perhaps through the protection afforded them by the extraordinary dimensions of the New World, to beat fate to the draw.

Karl Rossmann is truly innocent, and in this respect he differs radically from K., the protagonist of *The Trial* and *The Castle*. Whereas K., who is thoroughly impregnated with rationality, approaches the problem of guilt largely in a legalistic fashion, reacting vindictively to the misfortunes that befall him and seeking to prove by logical processes that he has committed no crime and should therefore be let alone, Karl suffers persecution without dreaming of vengeance or unduly dwelling on the wrongs

116

that have been done him. When his rich uncle wilfully turns him out of his house for virtually no reason at all, he utters no word of protest but calmly goes about the business of adjusting himself to his new situation. He is not a subjective character; his energy is of that benign kind which flows congenially even into the narrowest channels of reality.

The Kafkan irony expends itself on Karl by entangling him in a series of accidents, errors, and misunderstandings that are as circumstantially precise as they are magical in arrangement. His first steps in America—whose bewildering and immense bureaucratic mechanisms he dare not examine too closely—are attended by good fortune; but after a few months he is suddenly overtaken by disaster and compelled to take to the road in search of work in the company of the unemployed and thievish mechanics Delamarche and Robinson. After many trials he is befriended by a woman, a kind of Athene in the shape of a hotel manager. But this position too is soon lost to him, when he is abducted by the thievish mechanics with the design of forcing him into the service of Brunelda, a great slob of a Circe who had transformed them both into swinish lechers. (The seventh chapter, called "The Refuge," describing the Chaplinesque chase of Karl by a policeman, his encounter with the incomparable Brunelda, the election parade, and his conversation with the coffee-nourished student, is to my mind one of the finest single pieces of writing in modern fiction.) In the end he escapes from Brunelda's household to find work in the "Nature Theatre of Oklahoma," a beneficent and fantastic enterprise miraculously welcoming the unemployed into its almost limitless spaces, where they are provided with jobs and reconciled to the inscrutable purposes of the powers ruling the life of man.

Kafka makes no attempt to give a realistic account of America. He is quite inaccurate in every detail, yet the picture as a whole has uncanny symbolic truth. And if on its existential side this story is a sort of good-humored parody of the career of Poor Richard, on its literary side it derives from Dickens. David Copperfield, who is also a good boy with the wit to make the most of his virtue in his trials and tribulations, is Karl's prototype. But this "imitation" of Dickens' novel is in its way a burlesque treatment of it and is analogous to Joyce's use of Homer in his *Ulysses*.

One misses in *Amerika* the profound implications of Kafka's other work. Plainly his imagination did not wholly support this one effort to guide the life of a human being to a happy outcome. He was more at home in the dread castles and courts where K. wanders in search of justice, only to discover at the very last that justice is as meaningless as it is inescapable. *Amerika* belongs to what one might call the psychological phase of Kafka's art. The movement of this art is from psychology to experimental mythology, from the immediate appropriation of personal states to their projection into the world at large. Thus the principle of authority on which his work is grounded is at the outset, as in "The Judgment" and "The Metamorphosis," represented in the figure of a "real" father, a father whom it is not very difficult to identify in terms of the Freudian "family romance," while in the later and longer fictions the father is no longer recognizable as a figure in the world we know. He has been removed from the family circle and generalized into an institutional power—hierarchic, remote, mysterious—such as the Law, the Court and the order of officials that reside in the Castle.

In respect to this line of development "In the Penal Colony" can be regarded as a transitional story. It was written in November, 1914, when Kafka had already begun working on *The Trial*. Perhaps because it shows the influence of Kierkegaard, upon whom Kafka first came in 1913, the religious analogues of this story are clearer than in the earlier tales. The Old Commander, whose dread memory is invoked in "In the Penal Colony," retains some of the individual traits of the "real" father, at the same time as he is mythicized in the manner of the images of authority projected in the later novels.

But in the long run the early breakthrough in his writing to the deeper layers of his psychic life failed to free Kafka of his nerve-destroying fears and sense of unworthiness. He continued to quarrel with himself, plotting self-punishment, thinking even of suicide. "Balzac carried a cane on which was carved the legend: I smash every obstacle; my legend reads: Every obstacle smashes me." The constant seesaw between writing and his job affected his health. He suffered from headaches and insomnia, finally tuberculosis set in and he was compelled to spend years in sanitariums. His illness he considered to be psychically determined—"My head conspired with my lung behind my back." It was not until 1923, when he met Dora Dymant, a girl brought up in an orthodox Jewish family in Poland, and he found himself well enough to move with her to Berlin, that he at long last realized his longing for independence. But, as it turned out, it was already too late to obtain the restitution he sought for the lost years of sickness and misery. In June, 1924, at the age of forty-one, he died in a hospital near Vienna of laryngeal tuberculosis.

During his lifetime he published only some of his shorter works, and he never quite finished any of his three novels. Before his death he wrote to Max Brod requesting him to burn all the manuscripts he was leaving behind. Fortunately, his friend took upon himself the honorable responsibility of disregarding that desperate last instruction.

THE DEATH OF IVAN ILYICH
AND JOSEPH K.

Franz Kafka is best known for his innovations. His originality has so dazzled his readers that they tend to think of him almost solely in terms detached from any of the historic tendencies of modern literature. In recent years, however, we have learned to suspect excessive originality. The intensive study by modern critics of the relation between tradition and original talent has convinced most of us that originality at the point where it becomes the equivalent of eccentricity is more often a sign of weakness than of strength. In this sense, the isolation of Kafka not only delays a just estimate of his achievement but also exposes him to the danger that we shall merely gape at his phantastic performance and pass on.

The real question is whether Kafka's isolation is justified. Now while it is true that in certain respects Kafka is an idiosyncratic writer and that it would not do to underrate the extent to which he departed from the norms of the literary imagination, still it can be argued that the characteristic vision of his work is associated—at a level beyond surface "strangeness" or purely private inspiration—with other modern creations not generally regarded as unique or abnormal. This may be demonstrated by comparing Kafka's novel *The Trial* with Tolstoy's *The Death of Ivan Ilyich,* a shorter narrative more widely known perhaps than any of Kafka's writings. The two narratives, though quite dissimilar in their formal subject-matter and literary methods, seem to me essentially similar in theme and conception. Above all they share a common ideological tendency, which is objective in the sense that it exists on a social and historical rather than personal plane. This tendency can be defined as a tendency against scientific rationalism, against civilization, against the heresies of the man of the city whose penalty is spiritual death.

It is two works I am comparing, of course, not two writers. In the hierarchy of modern literary art Tolstoy obviously ranks higher than Kafka. Indeed, considered as creative personalities the two men are poles apart. One was an aristocratic yet elemental genius, whose initial identification with the natural world was more profound than his subsequent recoil from it; the other was an invalid and a neurotic, a prey to all the fears that beset the small, lost people of the city, who was driven by an obsessive feeling of guilt to burrow into the very foundations of reality. All the more startling, then, to hear the Tolstoyan cry from above, from the heights, also issuing from below, from the Kafkan underground.

It is not, of course, as an existential study of death that *Ivan Ilyich* falls into the same framework as *The Trial.* The Tolstoyan concern with mortality is not shared by Kafka, who found life so nearly impossible that he could hardly muster the strength to look beyond it. In associating the two narratives the first thing that comes to mind, rather, is their common religious basis, for both echo with the Augustinian imprecation, "Woe unto thee, thou stream of human custom!" But the religious basis, though important, is much too general and variable to serve directly as a unifying principle. Patently Tolstoy's system of Christian anarchism excludes Kafka's dominant hypothesis of the incommensurability of the human and divine orders. It is above all within the range of depicted experience, of the applied attitudes toward the real and the unreal, that the correspondence between the two works reveals itself most clearly.

In the midst of their ordinary, and, to them, wholly satisfactory lives, Ivan Ilyich and Joseph K. are stricken down by mysterious catastrophes. Just as K., failing to win his case in the unknown and unknowable Court which tries him on an unspecified charge, is finally executed, so Ilyich, failing to recover from an "unheard of" illness, which no doctor is able to diagnose, finally dies in agony after screaming incessantly for three days and three nights. The "case" and the "illness" are variations of the same device, which permits the author to play God so as to confront an ordinary, self-satisfied mortal with an extraordinary situation, to put to rout his confidence in reason and in the habitual limits of his consciousness, and in the end to destroy him utterly.

Incapable of distinguishing themselves either for good or evil, neither Ilyich nor K. are sinners in the accepted sense. Nevertheless the inquisitorial art of their authors burns them at the stake as heretics. And their heresy consists simply of their typicality.

Standardized urban men, K. and Ilyich are typical products of a quantitative civilization. Neither rich nor poor and at all times removed from any material or spiritual extremity, they conform to the conventions with the regularity of a law of nature. Both are professional men: K. a bank official and Ilyich a state functionary, member of the "Judicial Council." They aspire to and ordinarily succeed in leading a life of light-hearted agreeableness and decorum. The history of Ilyich, says Tolstoy, "was the simplest, the most ordinary, and the most awful." He marries and children are born to him; but inevitably husband and wife get to despise each other, she becoming steadily more ill-tempered, and he striving to make the relationship void by hiding behind his social and official duties.

K., on the other hand, like Kafka, is a bachelor. Necessarily so, for that is a telling item in Kafka's indictment of him—an indictment which on the human plane is in fact no indictment at all—thus causing unwary readers to consider him innocent—but which on another plane contributes to his guilt. Kafka's letters and diaries show him to have been continually haunted by the image of family life. Because of his personal deracination, he tended to idealize any human bond which rooted an individual in the community and supported him in his efforts to attain a status sanctified by the earthly as well as celestial powers. A projection of that side of his personality which Kafka wished to punish, K. concentrates within himself some of the faults of his author's condition and character, including the absence of family ties.

But from the chrysalis of the Kafkan self there also emerges another figure, who, by means of a psychic transformation, assumes the role of judge and avenger. This dread antagonist summarily lifts K. out of his rationalist sloth and plunges the metaphysical knife into his breast. However, this antagonist is not a character whom we can recognize, he is not a living actor in the drama of K.'s fate. He is, rather, a transcendental emanation taking shape in the actual plot of the novel, which is really a plot against K.'s life—and, in the last analysis, against the human faith in visible reality.

The catastrophe which overtakes K. is immaculately conceived, and thus much more mysterious in its nature than the one which Tolstoy inflicts upon Ilyich. Kafka clears in one bound the naturalist barrier to his symbolist art; and in so far as he describes everyday scenes and objects, he does so on his own terms, with the aim of producing effects of irony, contrast, and suspense. *The Trial* opens with the sentence: "Someone must have been telling lies about Joseph K., for without having done anything wrong he was arrested one fine morning." This beguilement of the reader continues throughout the story, and though before long he begins doubting the "realism" of what he is told, he is not resentful of having been taken in by a false show, but, on the contrary, finds himself yielding entirely to this mockery of the real.

Kafka unites within one framework the realistic and symbolic, the recognizable and mysterious, in a way that severs the continuity of assumption between author and reader which has in a short time made the most difficult modern works universally accessible. To read him rightly one has, as it were, to learn to read anew; and to feel at home in his world it is first necessary to grasp his fundamental attitude toward life. At bottom the reason his meaning is so illegible is that he viewed life as essentially illegible, incomprehensible; which does not mean, however, that he thought it meaningless. Having made his main premise the unknowability of the relations within which man lives, Kafka could permit himself a free range of hypotheses concerning their true character. His narratives are speculations translated into the language of the imagination; they are myths whose judicious, mock-scientific tonality at once dissociates them from the myth as an historical product. Experimental in tendency, they are not so much findings about reality as methods of exploring it. One might call them experimental myths. As meanings they move strictly in a circle, for they always return to their point of departure, namely, the uncertain, the unknown, the unfathomable. Hence their beginnings and ends are really identical: the origin and culmination of a Kafkan story tend to fuse in our minds into a single mystery. Obviously the myth as *procedure,* the myth as a technique of investigation, is the myth inverted, the myth standing on its head; and in demonstrating its uses Kafka achieved a new mutation in the art of prose fiction.

But Kafka's myths are not experimental in the sense of an inner lack of commitment; nor are they experimental in the sense of a playful tentativeness of design. In one

125

of his notebooks he gives us a clue to his intention. What he wished most, he writes, was to recreate life in such a way that "while still retaining its natural full-bodied rise and fall, it would simultaneously be recognized no less clearly as a nothing, a dream, a dim hovering. . . . Considered as a wish, somewhat as if one were to hammer together a table with a painful and methodical and technical efficiency, and simultaneously do nothing at all, and not in such a way that people would say: 'Hammering a table together is nothing to him,' but rather 'Hammering a table together is really hammering a table together to him, but at the same time it is nothing,' whereby certainly the hammering would become still bolder, still surer, still more real and, if you will, still more senseless."

Kafka realizes his wish. His forms dissolve the recognizable world even as they hold us to it by their matter-of-fact precision of detail. K. is persecuted by chimerical powers while he works at his desk in a bank, lives in an ordinary boarding-house on an ordinary street, and is subject to normal impressions and distractions. Kafka succeeds in joining the two planes, in "hammering" them together until both are equally real and yet equally unreal. His intrinsic ambivalence found here its ideal expression. His myths, though experimental, unfold like dreams, and like dreams they banish the sense of "perhaps" and are predominantly made up of visual images. Their terror is like nothing so much as the sensation of drowning; it is the terror of sinking so deeply into work-aday reality that, magically transformed, it turns into a dream, an illusion.

However, this illusion, this "nothing, dream, dim hovering," has a content. It is the cruel and unfathomable poetry of relations, the alchemy of fate. Phenomena are known, explicable—hence the naturalistic description of backgrounds—but relations are inexplicable and phantastic. These relations Kafka personifies with bold literalness in the form of a summary Court in perpetual session, a divine hierarchy, an irrational aggregate of rules and regulations known as the Law. Utterly alienated from nature, he sees everything in terms of society, which he conceives as the totality of being within which dwell both the known and unknown, the earthly and heavenly, the divine Law and the human litigant. Kafka's fear and its objects are in the main social; his divinities are phantastic personifications of irrational relationships chiefly rendered in the fear-and-dependence imagery of the Father.

In his stories the immemorial symbolism of the divine is inverted. Brightness, purity, immateriality—what reason is there to believe that these are really the attributes of Heaven? Instead Kafka houses his Court in a slum and fills the dilapidated rooms with bad air. Even the Castle, which is seen through a medieval haze, is in reality a squat office-building where the functionaries—the angels and demons—are preoccupied with writing letters and filing documents. It is both easy and difficult to handle these functionaries; there are no fixed principles for dealing with them. Beyond their zeal in behalf of the Law, they share all the vices of humanity; and like the sons of God mentioned in the Book of Genesis, they pursue the daughters of man.

The officials of the Law never go hunting for crime among the populace: they are simply drawn toward the guilty. No errors are possible, and if such errors do occur, who is finally to say that they are errors? And man is not tried by means of his high ambitions, by the foiling of his heroic designs, but on the level of a realistic humanism, by the failure of his effort to define his status in the community and win a measure of control over his social and personal destiny. What is particularly original here, as well as baffling of course, is the combination of the archaic and modern. Reviving the furies of antiquity, the fatality lurking at the roots of existence, Kafka at the same time contrives to enclose them within the prosaic framework of litigations, petty documented worries, and bureaucratic tedium.

The metaphysical end sought by Kafka is accomplished

127

by Tolstoy in a different way, for his realistic method is sober and "heavier." Whereas Kafka plays, as it were, both ends against the middle, Tolstoy always proceeds from the external to the internal. In his apartment, one day, Ilyich goes up a ladder to have some hangings draped, misses a step and slips; "but, like a strong and nimble person, he clung on, and only knocked his side against the corner of a frame. The bruised place ached, but it soon passed off." In time, however, he begins complaining of an uncomfortable feeling on the "left side" of his stomach, and soon we see him hovering over the edge of an abyss. While his world is falling apart, his physicians are engaged in balancing the probabilities "between a loose kidney, chronic catarrh, and appendicitis." They never manage to come to a decision; nor are they able to mitigate the patient's suffering, let alone save him from his fate. And as the story goes on, the disease which lays Ilyich low gradually loses its verisimilitude, until finally it takes on the form of an occult visitation. Manifestly in order to get the better of the accepted normality of the world, the naturalism of Tolstoy's narrative must come to an end at the precise point where the symbolism of Kafka's begins: at a crisis not only of conscience but of objective reality. The devised catastrophe must reach a dimension where normal explanations cease to operate. Only within that dimension can it function properly. At the close of his life Ilyich realizes that the horrible thing that goes on within him—the irresistible "It"—is at once a disease and yet not a disease. Is it not, after all, the voice of his soul, just as K.'s Court is perhaps nothing more than a machine of persecution invented by his alter ego to penalize K.'s death in life? (In one of his parables Kafka envisions a prisoner who, seeing a gallows being erected in the courtyard of his prison, "mistakenly" believes it is meant for him, and that night he slips out of his cell and hangs himself.) But this simple explanation holds only on the level of ordinary religious psychology, in the light of which the ordeals of Ilyich and K. merely illustrate once again

128

the eternal struggle between man's brute nature and his soul. The real problem, however, is to discover the particular meanings, social and historical, of Ilyich's contrite soul and K.'s machine of persecution.

In the loneliness of his pain Ilyich understands at last that his life had been trivial and disgusting. In this accounting which he gives to himself he thinks of what he now desires. To live and not to suffer, yes, but how? And his reply: "Why, live as I used to live before, happily and pleasantly," shows that as yet no real change has occurred in him. But during the last three days and nights he feels himself being thrust by an invisible force into a black sack; and his agony is due to his being in the black sack of course, and—"still more to not being able to get right into it." What hinders him from fully getting into the black sack? The pretense that his life had been good.—"That justification of his life held him fast and would not let him go forward, and it caused him more agony than all." Only on freeing himself of this pretense, of this illusion, does the terror of death leave him and he expires.

Morally, the death of K. duplicates the death of Ilyich. He, too, at first mistakes his apocalyptic fate, not perceiving the shape of a hidden god outlined in the petty event of his arrest. He expects to return to his normal state of well-being as soon as the matter of the absurd and obscure charge against him is cleared up. But after a few scuffles with the agents of the Court, he realizes the gravity of his situation and engages lawyers to defend him. These lawyers might as well be Ilyich's doctors. Both Ilyich and K. feel that their ostensible protectors are wasting time in irrelevant and supposedly scientific generalities, while they—patient and defendant—want to know only one thing: Is their condition serious?

Much like Ilyich, K. is impelled to give an accounting of his life, his case requiring, he decides, that he put it in the form of a written plea for justice containing a complete review of his career down "to the smallest actions and accidents formulated and examined from every

129

angle." And just as Ilyich can no longer keep his mind on his legal documents, but must ask everybody questions concerning sick people, recoveries and deaths, so K. is continually distracted from his duties at the bank by his need to hunt out other defendants and compare experiences with them. Tolstoy's description of Ilyich's mounting incapacity to cope with his daily routine in view of that "matter of importance" which he must constantly keep before him, forms an almost exact parallel to those scenes in *The Trial* when K. stands looking out of his office window, so overwhelmed by his "case" that he can no longer face his business callers. And toward the end— on the evening of his execution—as two men in frock coats and top hats who look like old-time tenors arrive to take him away, K. likewise contents himself with half-truths. Though he allows his warders to lead him off, still he is not entirely resigned but must make a last-minute attempt to shake them loose. He is half in and half out of the black sack. But finally he understands that there is nothing "heroic" in resistance: "I have always wanted to snatch at the world with twenty hands, and not for a very laudable motive either. That was wrong, and am I to show now that not even a whole year's struggle with my case has taught me anything? Am I to leave this world as a man who shies away from all conclusions?" And thinking of that High Court to which he had in vain striven to penetrate, he suffers the knife to be turned in him twice.

2

The use to which Kafka puts the categories of law in *The Trial* is to some extent analogous to Tolstoy's use of medicine in *Ivan Ilyich*. Representative disciplines, institutions, conspicuous structures erected by man's progress and science, law and medicine are fortresses against which those who spurn the authority of progress and science must take up arms. But the assault takes different forms. Whereas Tolstoy makes a frontal attack, openly jeering at the doctors for their silly airs and pose of omniscience, and even accusing them of lying, Kafka enters the fortress disguised as a friend. Emotionally ambivalent, he sympathizes at once with the divine judge and with the human defendant; hence even as he demonstrates the meaninglessness of the notion of justice he wears the mask of legality. His unusual irony converts juridical relations, which we are accustomed to think of as supremely rational, into the very medium of irrationality. K. discovers that the enactments and ordinances of the Court are not motivated by a love of order but by caprice and every kind of disorderly impulse. Bent on proving the disjunction between justice and necessity, human intention and destiny, Kafka created in his myth of the Law a wonderfully imaginative, albeit emotionally cruel, equivalent of a philosophical idea.

Against this Law, which abhors reason, it is impossible to revolt; nor are reforms to be thought of. Combined action of the defendants (the socialist recommendation) is out of the question, for "each case is judged on its own merits, the Court is very conscientious about that. . . ." The arbitrariness of the system of justice impells the accused men to suggest improvements, and that is one of the sources of their pathos. The only sensible thing to do is to adapt oneself to existing conditions. "This great organization remains . . . in a state of delicate equilibrium, and if someone took it upon himself to alter the disposition of things around him, he ran the risk of losing his footing and falling to destruction while the organization would simply right itself by some compensating reaction in another part of its machinery. . . ."

Manifestly in this scheme of things the outlook for social progress is entirely blank, and Kafka's acceptance of its perils is unconditional. True, it is an irrational world, but its irrationality, he suggests, is perhaps no more than the specific illusion, the particular distortion, inherent in the human perspective. "In the fight between you and the world back the world!" he wrote. Such "backing" must be understood as a derangement of the attitudes native to western literary art. This art has always pitted itself against the world, the heroes it created struck out and often conquered it, at the very least they protested against its injustices and insufficiencies. Kafka, on the other hand, refuses to cheat the world of its triumph, and the peculiarly austere tone of his prose evolves out of the tension between his sympathy for his heroes and the doom to which he consigns them.

This doom, articulated in narrative terms through the device of the mysterious catastrophe, requires that before the final blow is struck the victim be subjected to a process of dehumanization. If to be human is to be what K. and Ilyich are, then to dehumanize is to spiritualize them —such is the logic of this process. Kafka ensnares K. in the web of an inhuman law; Tolstoy, ever steadfast in his naturalism, crushes his victim physically. The latter method is simpler and entirely orthodox as religious procedure. Invoking as it does the old dualism of body and spirit, it suggests modern ideas as well, such as the idea of kinship between disease and spirit stressed by Nietzsche and in his wake by Thomas Mann. "Disease," writes Mann in his essay *Goethe and Tolstoy,* "has two faces and a double relation to man and his human dignity. On the one hand it is hostile; by overstressing the physical, by throwing man back upon his own body, it has a dehumanizing effect. On the other hand, it is possible to feel about illness as a highly dignified human phenomenon." And while it may be going too far, he adds, to claim that disease and spirit are identical, still the two conceptions have much in common. "For the spirit is pride; it is a willful denial and contradiction of nature; it is detachment, withdrawal, estrangement from her." Mann's observations are supported by Tolstoy's practice in *Ivan Ilyich.* The story, which has the qualities of a rite of purification, was published in 1886, several years after the author's "conversion"; and the disease which ravages Ilyich evidently represents Tolstoy's reaction against the natural world with which he formerly identified himself and his advance toward a rational religiosity and an ethical conception of social existence.

But *The Trial* is a purer, a more ideal instance of a magical rite. In the psychology of its author it is not difficult to recognize the symptoms of a compulsion-neurosis. The conscience-phobia, the morbid scruples and self-depreciation, the ceremonial "correctness" of behavior conceived as a supple bargaining, as a counterbalance to the threatening maneuvers of fate, the compensatory altruism and humility—all are obvious symptoms. Freud remarks that the primary obsessive actions of compulsion neurotics are "really altogether of a magical nature"; and in another context he notes that insofar as the neuroses are caricatures of social and cultural creations, the compulsion-neurosis is like a caricature of a religion. More: aside from sexual features the Freudian theory detects in this and similar neuroses a regression in time to the world-pictures of primitive men. The collective representations of the primitive are reproduced by the neurotic on a subjective and antisocial basis. Perhaps Kafka's conception of destiny may be understood in part as an example of this type of neurotic regression. His depiction of the Court, despite the modernity of its bureaucratic procedures, recalls us to remote and primordial ideas of fate. This is even truer of his novel *The Castle,* where the sense of fate is expressed in spatial rather than in temporal terms. By this I mean that the Castle, which is the abode of divinity, as well as the village, which is the community of men—the crowd of celestial functionaries as well as the crowd of peasants—are all subordinate to an even more primary power which has no personification and no rationale but which is simply the necessary and eternal disposition of things. This conception of fate is older than religion and antedates the birth of the gods. It originated in the magical and animistic stage of tribal life. The Greek word *Moira*—fate—as F. M. Cornford has shown in his book *From Religion to Philosophy,* once

133

possessed spatial significance. It refers back to a cosmogony which was developed prior to the Homeric theogony. *Moira* was an impersonal potency dominating both gods and humans whose real meaning was portion, allotment, province, domain. To sin meant to enroach, to cross a sacred frontier, to expose oneself to Nemesis—the avenger of trespass. This "separation of the world into elemental provinces" can be traced back, according to Cornford, to the sanctification of "status," namely, to the projection into myth of the social and economic organization of the tribe.

In this sense it can be said that what is represented in *The Castle* is *Moira* rather than fate working itself out according to modern conceptions of it. Unable to establish himself in the "village," which is the province of man, the pathos of K. in this novel is the pathos of an alien whose pursuit of status ends in failure. Status is synonymous with the state of grace; and he who has a home has status. This home, this cosmic security, this sacred order of status, is not a mythical or psychological but an historical reality. It persisted as a way of life, despite innumerable modifications, until the bourgeois era, when the organization of human life on the basis of status was replaced by its organization on the basis of free contract. The new, revolutionary mode of production sundered the unity of the spiritual and temporal, converting all things into commodities and all traditional social bonds into voluntarily contracted relations. In this process man was despiritualized and society atomized; and it is against the background of this vast transformation of the social order that the meaning of the death of Ilyich and K. becomes historically intelligible.

What should be clearly understood about Ilyich and K. is that they typify the average man of modern society. Tolstoy was much more conscious of this than Kafka, who in picturing society as a fabulous totality confounded this world with the kingdom of heaven. But Tolstoy was socially motivated; his "conversion" was

134

prompted by the dissolution of the centuries-old feudal ties, the breakdown of the ancient patriarchal relations, and the protest of the bewildered peasantry and nobility against the transformation of Russia into a capitalist country. His preoccupation with religion mirrored a utopian social program which has been defined as "feudal socialism"; and the historically reversed socialism of an aristocracy which bankers and tradesmen threaten to evict or have evicted from power cannot but assume idealist and religious forms.

Ilyich is the man of the city—the anonymous commodity-materialist who sweeps away the simple and transparent social relations of the past. His energy, the depersonalized energy of the modern man, subverts the idyllic world of sanctified status. In this connection it is characteristic that the only positive figure in Tolstoy's story should be the peasant Gerasim, a domestic in Ilyich's household, whose health and heartiness, in contrast to that of the city people, not only does not offend but soothes the sick man. And as to the mysterious catastrophe which destroys Ilyich, what is it in historical reality if not the ghost of the old idealism of status returning to avenge itself on its murderer? Through Ilyich's death the expropriators are expropriated.

But Kafka's religious preoccupation, you will say, is devoid of social meaning, since it seems purely psychological and even neurotic in origin. Yes, but let us not confuse origin with content. While it is true that Kafka's religious feelings were fed by a neurosis, there is however a sense, I believe, in which one might speak of the modern neurotic as the victim of the destructive triumph of "psychology" over nature, of the city over the country. He might be described as a casualty of a collective neurosis, of an illness of society.

What is K. if not, again, the blank man of the city, the standard *Teilmensch* cut off from all natural ties? He lives in the agitated, ever changing world of modern relationships, a world in which the living man, destitute

135

of individuality, has forgotten the ancient poetry of status, the hallowed certitudes that once linked law and destiny, justice and necessity, rights and duties. It is this dry world and himself in it that Kafka represents in the person of K. Against him, who embodies the present, Kafka directs his irony by entangling him with the banished past, with the ancient poetry. This happens when K. is suddenly arrested by the agents of an unknown Court, and when he finds himself under the jurisdiction of an inaccessible Castle. The Court and the Castle are sinister symbols of the old idealism; and K.'s entanglement with it effects a phantastic reversal of past and present, or dream and reality. It is now the dream of the past which is installed as master, and reality—the present—is banished. Naturally, everything is now turned upside down for K. He, the perverted modern man, can never adapt himself to the conditions of the absolute; he commits the most ludicrous errors and, though guilty, he thinks himself innocent. As he enters the Court he feels stifled in its pure air; its magnificent chambers he mistakes for dingy tenement rooms. Blinded by the fierce light of *Moira,* he can never experience the unity of justice and necessity but must ever divide the one from the other. K. dies of his contact with the past. His fate bears witness to a conflict of past and present, a conflict out of which the past emerges victorious. But the victory is wholly metaphysical.

This analysis by no means implies that Kafka was in any way conscious of the hidden historic reference of his symbols. On the contrary, no one among modern writers seems more deficient in a sense of history. The conflict between past and present is rendered in his work as a conflict between the human and divine orders. K. is allowed to live out his illusions; in fact, on the human level he is justified, for on that level the Court inevitably appears to be no more than an arbitrary and amoral power. Nevertheless, since the divine disposition of things cannot ultimately be questioned, man is destined to be ever in the wrong. Yet this abstract and mystical idea cannot be taken at face value. The time-spirit enters art without waiting for the permission of the artist. Kafka was writing under an obscure and irresistible compulsion, and his attitude toward his work, which he seldom felt the need to publish, was contradictory: on the one hand he thought of it as a form of transcendental communion with his fellow-men, and on the other as an effort strictly personal in function. It would be short-sighted, however, to limit its application to its subjective origin and purpose.

So far as Kafka's religiosity is concerned, it is clear that he was not religious in any traditional sense. His imagination excluded dogmas, systems of theology, and the concept of time-hallowed institutions as a bulwark. He was not looking to religion to do the work of politics: to effect a new synthesis or restore an old one, to make culture coherent or to impose order upon society. His religious feeling was of a pristine nature, essentially magical and animistic; and he attempted to rematerialize the soul thousands of years after religious thought had dematerialized it.

Unlike novelists like Dostoevsky and even Tolstoy in some of his moods, who are seldom at a loss for directions to the divine, Kafka makes the unknowability of God his chief postulate and the lack of communication between man and the powers that rule him its first corollary. Whereas Dostoevsky does not at all hesitate to describe a saint, Kafka cannot even imagine saintliness, for that would imply familiarity with the divine—precisely what, in his view, is unattainable. He asked, What is God like? as if the conception of the deity is utterly without a history. And the phantasy of his interrogations on this theme is deepened by his turning the empirical method inside out in applying it to the investigation of a nonempirical hypothesis, to the rationalization of the irrational.

Moreover, to postulate a God without a history has its consequences: it means that one is also lifting the world out of history. And, indeed, in Kafka history is abolished; there is only one time, the present; his people are not characters but simply bundles of human behavior, as immutable as a dream, rendered instantaneously, their inner and outer selves confounded. Character, individuation, are after all a proof of some measure of adjustment to the environment; the Kafkan man, however, is deprived of the most elementary requisites of adjustment: he moves within the dimension of fate, never within the dimension of personality, and the necessary link between the two is sprung.

Yet in spite of the profoundly unhistorical character of Kafka's art there are certain qualities in K., the chief protagonist of his narratives, that cannot be perceived except on the plane of historical interpretation. Thus historically his death, as that of Ilyich, signifies the disappearance of the hero from the drama of fate; their death falls outside the framework of the traditional tragic scheme. Tragedy implies that the hero, though vanquished by fate, commemorates in his very defeat the greatness and importance of man. The hero is always sharply individualized; his is an ample character. The opposite is true of K. and Ilyich, however. They are characterless in the sense indicated by Dostoevsky when he wrote in *Notes from Underground* that "the man of the nineteenth century must be, is morally obliged to be, a characterless individual," and by Marx when he remarked that the advantages of progress are paid for by the loss of character.

K. and Ilyich are heroes neither on the classic nor on the romantic level. Romanticism made of the self the primary criterion of values and its hero relived the past in terms of the new, critical, self-conscious bourgeois individuality. But in time the abstract modes of modern life undermined the self-confidence of the romantic hero and, stripped of his hopes and ambitions, he sank into anonymity. It is this historic depletion of man which is brought to light in the fate of K. and Ilyich alike.

138

But whereas the pathos of Tolstoy is that of an heroic struggle for a better life and for a constructive, even if utopian, rationality in the perception of man's enterprises and fate, the pathos of Kafka is that of loneliness and exclusion. In him the tradition of western individualism regards itself with self-revulsion; its joyous, ruthless hero is now a victim; he who once proudly disposed of many possessions is now destitute, he has neither woman nor child; in his conflict with society he has suffered an utter rout, and his fate no longer issues from his own high acts but from the abstract, enigmatical relations that bend him to their impersonal will.

Despite his longing for positive values, Kafka never resolved his perplexity. Considered in purely subjective terms, his myth of the Law is clearly the idealized impasse of his experience. If in the past of humanity the *unknown*—God, Destiny, the law—served in the hands of kings and prophets as a collective and collectivizing formula, as an instrument of ordering and controlling life, in Kafka it manifests itself in an exhausted condition, no longer a means of mythically unifying reality but of decomposing it. The pious emotion is here being reabsorbed into its primordial origins. Again the gods are taboo, that is, both holy and unclean. Moreover, even they are unable to retrace their steps and go back to their ancient home in nature. Once the lively and fertile emanations of primitive fear, of tribal need and desire, they now exist only as dead letters in a statute-book.

Believing as he does in the spirituality of life, in the "indestructible," Kafka nevertheless replies to his own query about the coming of the Messiah by declaring that he will appear only "when he is no longer needed, he will arrive the day after his arrival, he will not come on the last of the days, but on the day after the last." So out of his reach is human fulfillment that it has become unreal. Even his hope for salvation is ambiguous. He fears it as the final betrayal, the ironic confirmation of his despair.

139

NOTES ON THE DECLINE
OF NATURALISM

Quite a few protests have been aired in recent years against the sway of the naturalist method in fiction. It is charged that this method treats material in a manner so flat and external as to inhibit the search for value and meaning, and that in any case, whatever its past record, it is now exhausted. Dissimilar as they are, both the work of Franz Kafka and the works of the surrealist school are frequently cited as examples of release from the routines of naturalist realism, from its endless bookkeeping of existence. Supporting this indictment are mostly those writers of the younger group who are devoted to experimentation and who look to symbolism, the fable, and the myth.

The younger writers are stirred by the ambition to create a new type of imaginative prose into which the recognizably real enters as one component rather than as the total substance. They want to break the novel of its objective habits; some want to introduce into it philosophical ideas; others are not so much drawn to expressing ideas as to expressing the motley strivings of the inner self—dreams, visions, and fantasies. Manifestly the failure of the political movement in the literature of the past decade has resulted in a revival of religio-esthetic attitudes.

141

The young men of letters are once again watching their own image in the mirror and listening to inner promptings. Theirs is a program calling for the adoption of techniques of planned derangement as a means of cracking open the certified structure of reality and turning loose its latent energies. And surely one cannot dispose of such a program merely by uncovering the element of mystification in it. For the truth is that the artist of the avant-garde has never hesitated to lay hold of the instruments of mystification when it suited his purpose, especially in an age such as ours, when the life about him belies more and more the rational ideals of the cultural tradition.

It has been remarked that in the long run the issue between naturalism and its opponents resolves itself into a philosophical dispute concerning the nature of reality. Obviously those who reject naturalism in philosophy will also object to its namesake in literature. But it seems to me that when faced with a problem such as that of naturalist fiction, the critic will do well not to mix in ontological maneuvers. From the standpoint of critical method it is impermissible to replace a concrete literary analysis with arguments derived from some general theory of the real. For it is plainly a case of the critic not being able to afford metaphysical commitments if he is to apply himself without preconceived ideas to the works of art that constitute his material. The art-object is from first to last the one certain datum at his disposal; and in succumbing to metaphysical leanings—either of the spiritualist or materialist variety—he runs the risk of freezing his insights in some kind of ideational schema the relevance of which to the task in hand is hardly more than speculative. The act of critical evaluation is best performed in a state of *ideal aloofness* from abstract systems. Its practitioner is not concerned with making up his mind about the ultimate character of reality but with observing and measuring its actual proportions and combinations within a given form. The presence of the real affects him di-

142

rectly, with an immediate force contingent upon the degree of interest, concreteness, and intensity in the impression of life conveyed by the literary artist. The philosopher can take such impressions or leave them, but luckily the critic has no such choice.

Imaginative writing cannot include fixed and systematic definitions of reality without violating its own existential character. Yet in any imaginative effort that which we mean by the real remains the basic criterion of viability, the crucial test of relevance, even if its specific features can hardly be determined in advance but must be *felt anew* in each given instance. And so far as the medium of fiction is concerned, one cannot but agree with Henry James that it gains its "air of reality"—which he considers to be its "supreme virtue"—through "its immense and exquisite correspondence with life." Note that James's formulation allows both for analogical and realistic techniques of representation. He speaks not of copies or reports or transcripts of life but of relations of equivalence, of a "correspondence" which he identifies with the "illusion of life." The ability to produce this illusion he regards as the storyteller's inalienable gift, "the merit on which all other merits . . . helplessly and submissively depend." This insight is of an elementary nature and scarcely peculiar to James alone, but it seems that its truth has been lost on some of our recent catch-as-catch-can innovators in the writing of fiction.

It is intrinsically from this point of view that one can criticize the imitations of Kafka that have been turning up of late as being one-sided and even inept. Perhaps Kafka is too idiosyncratic a genius to serve as a model for others, but still it is easy to see where his imitators go wrong. It is necessary to say to them: To know how to take apart the recognizable world is not enough, is in fact merely a way of letting oneself go and of striving for originality at all costs. But originality of this sort is nothing more than a professional mannerism of the avant-garde. The genuine innovator is always trying to make us actually experience his creative conflict. He therefore employs means that are subtler and more complex: *at the very same time that he takes the world apart he puts it together again.* For to proceed otherwise is to dissipate rather than alter our sense of reality, to weaken and compromise rather than change in any significant fashion our feeling of relatedness to the world. After all, what impressed us most in Kafka is precisely this power of his to achieve a simultaneity of contrary effects, to fit the known into the unknown, the actual into the mythic and vice versa, to combine within one framework a conscientiously empirical account of the visibly real with a magical decomposition of it. In this paradox lies the pathos of his approach to human existence.

A modern poetess has written that the power of the visible derives from the invisible; but the reverse of this formula is also true. Thus the visible and the invisible might be said to stand to each other in an ironic relation of inner dependence and of mutual skepticism mixed with solicitude. It is a superb form of doubletalk; and if we are accustomed to its exclusion from naturalistic writing, it is all the more disappointing to find that the newly evolved "fantastic" style of the experimentalists likewise excludes it. But there is another consideration, of a more formal nature. It seems to me a profound error to conceive of reality as merely a species of material that the fiction-writer can either use or dispense with as he sees fit. It is a species of material, of course, and something else besides: it also functions as the *discipline of fiction,* much in the same sense that syllabic structure functions as the discipline of verse. This seeming identity of the formal and substantial means of narrative prose is due, I think, to the altogether free and open character of the medium, which prevents it from developing such distinctly technical controls as poetry has acquired. Hence even the dream, when told in a story, must partake of some of the qualities of the real.

Whereas the surrealist represents man as immured in

144

dreams, the naturalist represents him in a continuous waking state of prosaic daily living, in effect as never dreaming. But both the surrealist and the naturalist go to extremes in simplifying the human condition. J. M. Synge once said that the artist displays at once the difficulty and the triumph of his art when picturing the dreamer leaning out to reality or the man of real life lifted out of it. "In all the poets," he wrote, and this test is by no means limited to poetry alone, "the greatest have both these elements, that is they are supremely engrossed with life, and yet with the wildness of their fancy they are always passing out of what is simple and plain."

The old egocentric formula, "Man's fate is his character," has been altered by the novelists of the naturalist school to read, "Man's fate is his environment." (Zola, the organizer and champion of the school, drew his ideas from physiology and medicine, but in later years his disciples cast the natural sciences aside in favor of the social sciences.) To the naturalist, human behavior is a function of its social environment; the individual is the live register of its qualities; he exists in it as animals exist in nature.* Due to this emphasis the naturalist mode has

---

* Balzac, to whom naturalism is enormously indebted, explains in his preface to the *Comédie Humaine* that the idea of that work came to him in consequence of a "comparison between the human and animal kingdoms." "Does not society," he asks, "make of man, in accordance with the environment in which he lives and moves, as many different kinds of man as there are different zoological species? . . . There have, therefore, existed and always will exist social species, just as there are zoological species."
Zola argues along the same lines: "All things hang together: it is necessary to start from the determination of inanimate bodies in order to arrive at the determination of living beings; and since savants like Claude Bernard demonstrate now that fixed laws govern the human body, we can easily proclaim . . . the hour in which the laws of thought and passion will be formulated in their turn. A like determination will govern the stones of the roadway and the brain of man.

evolved historically in two main directions. On the one hand it has tended towards passive documentation (milieu-panoramas, local-color stories, reportorial studies of a given region or industry, etc.), and on the other towards the exposure of socio-economic conditions (muckraking). American fiction of the past decade teems with examples of both tendencies, usually in combination. The work of James T. Farrell, for instance, is mostly a genre-record, the material of which is in its very nature operative in producing social feeling, while such novels as *The Grapes of Wrath* and *Native Son* are exposure-literature, as is the greater part of the fiction of social protest. Dos Passos' trilogy, *U. S. A.*, is thoroughly political in intention but has the tone and gloss of the methodical genre-painter in the page by page texture of its prose.

I know of no hard and fast rules that can be used to distinguish the naturalist method from the methods of realism generally. It is certainly incorrect to say that the difference is marked by the relative density of detail. Henry James observes in his essay *The Art of Fiction* that it is above all "solidity of specification" that makes for the illusion of life—the air of reality in a novel; and the truth of this dictum is borne out by the practice of the foremost modern innovators in this medium, such as Proust, Joyce, and Kafka. It is not, then, primarily the means employed to establish verisimilitude that fix the naturalist imprint upon a work of fiction. A more conclusive test, to my mind, is its treatment of the relation of character to background. I would classify as naturalistic that type of realism in which the individual is portrayed not merely as subordinate to his background but as wholly determined by it—that type of realism, in other words, in which the environment displaces its inhabitants in the role of the hero. Theodore Dreiser, for example, comes as close as any American writer to plotting the

. . . We have experimental chemistry and medicine and physiology and later on an experimental novel. It is an inevitable evolution." (*The Experimental Novel*)

careers of his characters strictly within a determinative process. The financier Frank Cowperwood masters his world and emerges as its hero, while the "little man" Clyde Griffiths is the victim whom it grinds to pieces; yet hero and victim alike are essentially implements of environmental force, the carriers of its contradictions upon whom it stamps success or failure—not entirely at will, to be sure, for people are marked biologically from birth —but with sufficient autonomy to shape their fate.

In such a closed world there is patently no room for the singular, the unique, for anything in fact which cannot be represented plausibly as the product of a particular social and historical complex. Of necessity the naturalist must deal with experience almost exclusively in terms of the broadly typical. He analyzes characters in such a way as to reduce them to standard types. His method of construction is that of accretion and enumeration rather than of analysis or storytelling; and this is so because the quantitative development of themes, the massing of detail and specification, serves his purpose best. He builds his structures out of literal fact and precisely documented circumstance, thus severely limiting the variety of creative means at the disposal of the artist.

This quasi-scientific approach not only permits but, in theory at least, actually prescribes a neutral attitude in the sphere of values. In practice, however, most naturalists are not sufficiently detached or logical to stay put in such an ultraobjective position. Their detractors are wrong in denying them a moral content; the most that can be said is that theirs is strictly functional morality, bare of any elements of gratuity or transcendence and devoid of the sense of personal freedom.* Clearly such a perspective allows for very little self-awareness on the part of characters. It also removes the possibility of a tragic resolution of experience. The world of naturalist fiction is much too big, too inert, too hardened by social

---

* Chekhov remarks in one of his stories that "the sense of personal freedom is the chief constituent of creative genius."

habit and material necessity, to allow for that tenacious self-assertion of the human by means of which tragedy justifies and ennobles its protagonists. The only grandeur naturalism knows is the grandeur of its own methodological achievement in making available a vast inventory of minutely described phenomena, in assembling an enormous quantity of data and arranging them in a rough figuration of reality. *Les Rougon-Macquart* stands to this day as the most imposing monument to this achievement.

But in the main it is the pure naturalist—that monstrous offspring of the logic of a method—that I have been describing here. Actually no such literary animal exists. Life always triumphs over methods, over formulas and theories. There is scarcely a single novelist of any importance wearing the badge of naturalism who is all of a piece, who fails to compensate in some way for what we miss in his fundamental conception. Let us call the roll of the leading names among the French and American naturalists and see wherein each is saved.

The Goncourts, it is true, come off rather badly, but even so, to quote a French critic, they manage "to escape from the crude painting of the naked truth by their impressionistic mobility" and, one might add, by their mobile intelligence. Zola's case does not rest solely on our judgment of his naturalist dogmas. There are entire volumes by him—the best, I think, is *Germinal*—and parts of volumes besides, in which his naturalism, fed by an epic imagination, takes on a mythic cast. Thomas Mann associates him with Wagner in a common drive toward an epic mythicism:

They belong together. The kinship of spirit, method, and aims is most striking. This lies not only in the ambition to achieve size, the propensity to the grandiose and the lavish; nor is it the Homeric leitmotiv alone that is common to them; it is first and foremost a special kind of naturalism, which develops into the mythical. . . . In Zola's epic . . . the characters themselves are raised up to a plane above that of every day. And is that Astarte of the Second Empire, called Nana,

148

not symbol and myth? (*The Sufferings and Greatness of Richard Wagner*)

Zola's prose, though not controlled by an artistic conscience, overcomes our resistance through sheer positiveness and expressive energy—qualities engendered by his novelistic ardor and avidity for recreating life in all its multiple forms.* As for Huysmans, even in his naturalist period he was more concerned with style than with subject-matter. Maupassant is a naturalist mainly by alliance, i.e., by virtue of his official membership in the School of Médan; actually he follows a line of his own, which takes off from naturalism never to return to it. There are few militant naturalists among latter-day French writers. Jules Romains is sometimes spoken of as one, but the truth is that he is an epigone of all literary doctrines, including his own. Dreiser is still unsurpassed so far as American naturalism goes, though just at present he may well be the least readable. He has traits that make for survival—a Balzacian grip on the machinery of money and power; a prosiness so primary in texture that if taken in bulk it affects us as a kind of poetry of the commonplace and ill-favored; and an emphatic eroticism which is the real climate of existence in his fictions— Eros hovering over the shambles. Sinclair Lewis was never a novelist in the proper sense that Zola and Dreiser are novelists, and, given his gift for exhaustive reporting, naturalism did him more good than harm by providing him with a ready literary technique. In Farrell's chronicles there is an underlying moral code which, despite his explicit rejection of the Church, seems to me indisputably orthodox and Catholic; and his Studs Lonigan—a product of those unsightly urban neighborhoods where youth prowls and fights to live up to the folk-ideal of the "regular guy"—is no mere character but an archetype,

---

* Moreover, it should be evident that Zola's many faults are not rectified but merely inverted in much of the writing—so languidly allusive and decorative—of the literary generations that turned their backs on him.

an eponymous hero of the street-myths that prevail in our big cities. The naturalism of Dos Passos is most completely manifested in *U. S. A.*, tagged by the critics as a "collective" novel recording the "decline of our business civilization." But what distinguishes Dos Passos from other novelists of the same political animus is a sense of justice so pure as to be almost instinctive, as well as a deeply elegiac feeling for the intimate features of American life and for its precipitant moments. Also, *U. S. A.* is one of the very few naturalist novels in which there is a controlled use of language, in which a major effect is produced by the interplay between story and style. It is necessary to add, however, that the faults of Dos Passos' work have been obscured by its vivid contemporaneity and vital political appeal. In the future, I think, it will be seen more clearly than now that it dramatizes social symptoms rather than lives and that it fails to preserve the integrity of personal experience. As for Faulkner, Hemingway, and Caldwell, I do not quite see on what grounds some critics and literary historians include them in the naturalist school. I should think that Faulkner is exempted by his prodigious inventiveness and fantastic humor. Hemingway is a realist on one level, in his attempts to catch the "real thing, the sequence of motion and fact which made the emotion"; but he is also subjective, given to self-portraiture and to playing games with his ego; there is very little study of background in his work, a minimum of documentation. In his best novels Caldwell is a writer of rural abandon—and comedy. His Tobacco Road is a sociological area only in patches; most of it is exotic landscape.

It is not hard to demonstrate the weakness of the naturalist method by abstracting it, first, from the uses to which individual authors put it and, second, from its function in the history of modern literature. The traditionalist critics judge it much too one-sidedly in professing to see in its rise nothing but spiritual loss—an invasion of the arcanum of art by arid scientific ideas. The point is that this scientific bias of naturalism was historically productive of contradictory results. Its effect was certainly depressive insofar as it brought mechanistic notions and procedures into writing. But it should be kept in mind that it also enlivened and, in fact, revolutionized writing by liquidating the last assets of "romance" in fiction and by purging it once and for all of the idealism of the "beautiful lie"—of the long-standing inhibitions against dealing with the underside of life, with those inescapable day-by-day actualities traditionally regarded as too "sordid" and "ugly" for inclusion within an aesthetic framework. If it were not for the service thus rendered in vastly increasing the store of literary material, it is doubtful whether such works as *Ulysses* and even *Remembrance of Things Past* could have been written. This is not clearly understood in the English speaking countries, where naturalism, never quite forming itself into a "movement," was at most only an extreme emphasis in the general onset of realistic fiction and drama. One must study, rather, the Continental writers of the last quarter of the nineteenth century in order to grasp its historical role. In discussing the German naturalist school of the 1880's, the historian Hans Naumann has this to say, for instance:

Generally it can be said that to its early exponents the doctrine of naturalism held quite as many diverse and confusing meanings as the doctrine of expressionism seemed to hold in the period just past. Imaginative writers who at bottom were pure idealists united with the dry-as-dust advocates of a philistine natural-scientific program on the one hand and with the shameless exploiters of erotic themes on the other. All met under the banner of naturalism—friends today and enemies tomorrow. . . . But there was an element of historical necessity in all this. The fact is that the time had come for an assault, executed with glowing enthusiasm, against the epigones . . . that it was finally possible to fling aside with disdain and anger the pretty falsehoods of life and art (*Die Deutsche Dichtung der Gegenwart*, Stuttgart, 1930, p. 144).

And he adds that the naturalism of certain writers consisted simply in their "speaking honestly of things that had heretofore been suppressed."

But to establish the historical credit of naturalism is not to refute the charges that have been brought against it in recent years. For whatever its past accomplishments, it cannot be denied that its present condition is one of utter debility. What was once a means of treating material truthfully has been turned, through a long process of depreciation, into a mere convention of truthfulness, devoid of any significant or even clearly definable literary purpose or design. The spirit of discovery has withdrawn from naturalism; it has now become the common denominator of realism, available in like measure to the producers of literature and to the producers of kitsch. One might sum up the objections to it simply by saying that it is no longer possible to use this method *without taking reality for granted*. This means that it has lost the power to cope with the ever growing element of the problematical in modern life, which is precisely the element that is magnetizing the imagination of the true artists of our epoch. Such artists are no longer content merely to question particular habits or situations or even institutions; it is reality itself which they bring into question. Reality to them is like that "open wound" of which Kierkegaard speaks in his *Journals*: "A healthy open wound; sometimes it is healthier to keep a wound open; sometimes it is worse when it closes."

There are also certain long-range factors that make for the decline of naturalism. One such factor is the growth of psychological science and, particularly, of psychoanalysis. Through the influence of psychology literature recovers its inwardness, devising such forms as the interior monologue, which combines the naturalistic in its minute description of the mental process with the anti-naturalistic in its disclosure of the subjective and the irrational. Still another factor is the tendency of naturalism, as Thomas Mann observes in his remarks on Zola, to turn into the mythic through sheer immersion in the typical. This dialectical negation of the typical is apparent in a work like *Ulysses,* where "the myth of the *Odyssey,*" to quote from Harry Levin's study of Joyce, "is superimposed upon the map of Dublin" because only a myth could "lend shape or meaning to a slice of life so broad and banal." And from a social-historical point of view this much can be said, that naturalism cannot hope to survive the world of nineteenth-century science and industry of which it is the product. For what is the crisis of reality in contemporary art if not at bottom the crisis of the dissolution of this familiar world? Naturalism, which exhausted itself taking an inventory of this world while it was still relatively stable, cannot possibly do justice to the phenomena of its disruption.

One must protest, however, against the easy assumption of some avant-gardist writers that to finish with naturalism is the same as finishing with the principle of realism generally. It is one thing to dissect the real, to penetrate beneath its faceless surface and transpose it into terms of symbol and image; but the attempt to be done with it altogether is sheer regression or escape. Of the principle of realism it can be said that it is the most valuable acquisition of the modern mind. It has taught literature how to take in, how to grasp and encompass, the ordinary facts of human existence; and I mean this in the simplest sense conceivable. Least of all can the novelist dispense with it, as his medium knows of no other principle of coherence. In Gide's *Les Faux-Monnayeurs* there is a famous passage in which the novelist Edouard enumerates the faults of the naturalist school. "The great defect of that school is that it always cuts a slice of life in the same direction: in time, lengthwise. Why not in breadth? Or in depth? As for me, I should like not to cut at all. Please understand: I should like to put everything into my novel." "But I thought," his interlocutor remarks, "that you want to abandon reality." Yes,

153

replies Edouard, "my novelist wants to abandon it; but I shall continually bring him back to it. In fact that will be the subject; the struggle between the facts presented by reality and the ideal reality."

I. DR. WILLIAMS IN
HIS SHORT STORIES

In his prose as in his poetry William Carlos Williams is too hardy a frontiersman of the word to permit himself the idle luxuries of aestheticism. There are too many things to be seen and touched, too many cadences of living speech to be listened to and recorded. Kenneth Burke once said of Williams that he was engaged in "discovering the shortest route between subject and object." Perhaps that explains why in *Life on the Passaic River,* a collection of nineteen short stories, not one imitates in any way the conventional patterns of the genre. The directness of this writer's approach to his material excludes its subjection to the researches of plot and calculated form. What Williams tells us is much too close to him to lend itself to the alienation of design; none of his perceptions can be communicated through the agency of invented equivalents. The phenomena he observes and their meanings are so intimately involved with one another, the cohabitation of language and object is so harmonious, that formal means of expression would not only be superfluous but might actually nullify the incentive to creation.

These notations in a doctor's notebook, these fragments salvaged from grime and squalor, these insights gained during the routines of humble labor—such would only be given the lie by the professional mannerisms of authorship, its pomposities and braggadocio. Where a writer usually takes the attitude of an impresario toward his themes, calculating each entrance and exit, Williams will begin or end his story as the spirit moves him; pausing to face his reader, he will take him into his confidence and speak his mind without recourse to stratagems of ingratiation. Elliptical in some passages and naturalistic in others, Williams is perfectly conscious of writing but hostile to "literature." Out of "a straight impulse, without borrowing, without lie or complaint," he puts down on paper that which stirs him. His subjects are few and often minute, their scope is sharply circumscribed by his personal experience and by his voluntary seclusion within the local and immediate, he repeats himself frequently—yet these stories are exceptional for their authenticity and told not to provoke but to record. It is pain which is the source of values here. The dread of annihilation is ever present. "Christ, Christ! . . . How can a man live in the face of this daily uncertainty? How can a man not go mad with grief, with apprehension?" No grand conceits, no gratuitous excitements, no melodrama. There is no doing away with the staples of existence; no gallivanting on the banks of the Passaic River.

For what could be more dismal than life in these small industrial towns of New Jersey? The mills are worked by immigrant laborers, and their youngsters are "all over the city as soon as they can walk and say, Paper!" The doctor visits these uprooted households, often angry at himself because of the tenderness in him that reaches out to these people, quite as often resigned to doing his job, to immersing himself in the finalities of human life. "To me," he writes, "it is a hard, barren life, where I am alone and unmolested (work as I do in the thick of it), though in constant danger lest some slip send me to perdition but which, being covetous not at all, I enjoy for the seclusion and primitive air of it."

The little girl, both of whose tonsils are covered with membrane, fights furiously to keep him from knowing her secret. Another one, a lank-haired girl of fifteen, is a powerful little animal upon whom you can stumble on the roof, behind the stairs "any time at all." A whole gang is on her trail. Cured of her pimples, how will this tenacious creature ever slash her way to the bliss recited on the radio? "The pure products of America go crazy," Williams once wrote in a poem. And these stories are familiar images of the same, released by that active element of sympathy which is to be prized above all else in the equipment of an artist. But this writer has no hankering for consistent explanations, for the constancy of reason; he seldom permits himself to ask why. "What are you going to do with a guy like that. Or why want to do anything with him. Except not miss him," he says of one of his characters. This last is the point. He is content with grasping the fact, with creating a phenomenology; but the relations, social and historic, that might unify these facts and significate them on a plane beyond sensation or nostalgia or pathos he has no mind for. And this absence of what one might call, in his terms, ideological presumptuousness, while admirable in its modesty, also constitutes his defeat. However much of value there is in these facts of "hard history" and in the scrupulous gathering of their detail, the larger implications are systematically neglected. Thought is proscribed as anti-aesthetic. Yet, though habitually confined to the suggestive and purely descriptive, this prose nevertheless holds within itself some of the raw elements of a comprehensive consciousness.

But Williams does think about America, if only to sketch it in psychic outline. He is under the spell of its *mystique* and strains to encompass it in a vision. This need in him provides a contrast and relief to the phenomenological principle informing his work; and much of his charm flows from the interaction of his precise facts with his American mysticism. In his novel, *White Mule,* the fusion of these two qualities allowed a visible direction to

157

emerge. "What then is it like, America?" asks Fraulein Von J. in "The Venus," which seems to me the best story in the collection. This German girl is a genuine Weimar-period object. She has a genius for formulating the most complex modern problems in the simplest terms. The daughter of a general, she comes to Italy to become a nun. But perhaps America—she questions the American, Evans, who carries a flint arrowhead in his pocket—could prove a satisfactory alternative to the Church? Evans speaks of the old pioneer houses of his ancestors, and of that "early phase" of America whose peculiar significance has been forgotten or misunderstood. The German girl holds the arrowhead in her hand, feeling its point and edge. "It must be even more lonesome and frightening in America than in Germany," she finally says. The story recalls us to the Williams of *In the American Grain,* a writer ravaged by this hemisphere's occult aboriginal past. In some ways Dr. Williams is really a medicine-man.

1938

II. HENRY MILLER

If Henry Miller's status in our literary community is still so very debatable, it is probably because he is the type of writer who cannot help exposing himself to extreme appraisals with every page that he adds to his collected works. He is easily overrated and with equal ease run down or ignored altogether. Consider his present situation. With few exceptions the highbrow critics, bred almost to a man in Eliot's school of strict impersonal aesthetics, are bent on snubbing him. What with his spellbinder's tone, bawdy rites, plebeian rudeness and disdain of formal standards, he makes bad copy for them and they know it. His admirers, on the other hand, are so hot-lipped in praise as to arouse the suspicion of a cultist attachment. They evade the necessity of drawing distinctions between the art of exploiting one's personality and the art of exploiting material, from whatever source, for creative purposes. And in Miller's case such distinctions are very much in order. His work is so flagrantly personal in content that in moments of acute irritation one is tempted to dismiss it as so much personality-mongering. Repeatedly he has declared that his concern is not with writing as generally understood but with telling the "more and more inexhaustible" story of his life—a story stretched to include a full recital of his opinions, philosophic rhapsodies, intuitions, hunches, and buffooneries. All too often he plunges into that maudlin boosting of the ego to which the bohemian character is generically disposed. Yet at his best he writes on a level of true expressiveness, generating a kind of all-out poetry, at once genial and savage.

Unfortunately, since finishing off his expatriation and returning to his native country he has given more and more free rein to his worst tendency, that of playing the philosopher on a binge and the gadabout of the California avant-garde. The last book of his in which his great talent is shown to best advantage is *The Colossus of Maroussi,* published in 1942. It is a travel book on Greece of a very special type. Though containing some plain information about the country and its inhabitants, it intrinsically belongs to the modern tradition of the fugitives from progress—from the lands ravaged by the machine, the salesman, and the abstract thinker—the tradition of Melville and Gauguin in Tahiti and D. H. Lawrence in Mexico and Taos. Miller went to Greece to purge himself of his long contact with the French and to make good his hope for spiritual renewal. "In Greece," he writes, "I finally achieved coordination. I became deflated, restored to proper human proportions, ready to accept my lot and to give of all that I have received. Standing in Agamemnon's tomb I went through a veritable rebirth." He speaks of the Greeks as "aimless, anarchic, thoroughly and discordantly human," thus identifying them closely with his own values; and though confessing that he never read a line of Homer, he none the less believes them to be essentially unchanged.

Where he shows an unusual aptitude for descriptive prose is in the account of his visits to Mycenae, Knossus, Phaestos, and other sites of antiquity. Some of the passages are very good examples of his rhetorical prowess. Hyperbolic statement is his natural mode of communication, yet he has a vital sense of reference to concrete objects and symbols which permits him to gain a measure of

160

control over his swelling language. He is particularly addicted to using terms and images drawn from science, especially biology and astronomy; and his unvarying practice is to distribute these borrowings stylistically in a manner so insinuating as to produce effects of incongruity and alarm. It is a device perfectly expressive of his fear of science and all its works. For Miller belongs to the progress-hating and machine-smashing fraternity of contemporary letters, though lacking as he does the motive of allegiance to tradition, it is open to question whether his co-thinkers would ever assent to his company. Of late, too, he has increasingly yielded to his mystical leanings, and his mysticism is of the wholesale kind, without limit or scruple. Thus there is a curious chapter in *The Colossus of Maroussi* describing his interview with an Armenian soothsayer in Athens, who confirms Miller in his belief that he is never going to die and that he is destined to undertake missions of a messianic nature that will "bring great joy to the world." Now this is the sort of thing that can be taken, of course, either as a fancy piece of megalomania or as a legitimate aspiration to which every human being is entitled.

But if Miller's recent work has been disappointing, the one way to recover a sense of his significance is to go back to his three early novels—*Tropic of Cancer, Black Spring,* and *Tropic of Capricorn.* These novels are autobiographical, and he appears in them in the familiar role of the artist-hero who dominates modern fiction. Where he differs from this ubiquitous type is in the extremity of his destitution and estrangement from society. Reduced to the status of a lumpen-proletarian whom the desolation of the big city has finally drained of all illusions and ideals, he is now an utterly declassed and alienated man who lives his life in the open streets of Paris and New York.

In these novels the narrator's every contact with cultural objects serves merely to exacerbate his anarchic impulses.

There no longer exists for him any shelter from the external world. Even the idea of home—a place that the individual can truly call his own because it is furnished not only with his belongings but with his very humanity —has been obliterated. What remains is the fantasy of returning to the womb, a fantasy so obsessive as to give rise to an elaborate intra-uterine imagery as well as to any number of puns, jokes, imprecations, and appeals.

It is precisely in his descriptions of his lumpen-proletarian life in the streets that Miller is at his best, that his prose is most resonant and alive—the streets in which a never ending array of decomposed and erratic phenomena gives his wanderings in search of a woman or a meal the metaphysical sheen of dream and legend. In every shop-window he sees the "sea-nymph squirming in the maniac's arms," and everywhere he smells the odor of love "gushing like sewergas" out of the leading mains: "Love without gender and without lysol, incubational love, such as the wolverines practice above the treeline." In these novels food and sex are thematically treated with such matter-of-fact exactitude, with such a forceful and vindictive awareness of rock-bottom needs, that they cease to mean what they mean to most of us. Miller invokes food and sex as heroic sentiments and even generalizes them into principles. For the man who is down and out has eyes only for that which he misses most frequently; his condition makes of him a natural anarchist, rendering irrelevant all conventions, moral codes, or any attempt to order the process of experience according to some value-pattern. The problem is simply to keep alive, and to that end all means are permissible. One turns into a desperado, lurking in ambush in hallways, bars, and hotel rooms in the hope that some stroke of luck will enable one "to make a woman or make a touch." He literally takes candy from babies and steals money from prostitutes. As for obtaining regular work, he was always able "to amuse, to nourish, to instruct, but never to be accepted in a genuine way . . . everything conspired to set me off as an *outlaw*."

The fact that the world is in a state of collapse fills him with deep gratification ("I am dazzled by the glorious collapse of the world") because the all-around ruin seems to justify and validate what has happened to him personally. His particular adjustment he accomplishes by accepting the collapse as a kind of apocalyptic show from which the artist who has been rejected by society, and whose role is to revive the primeval, chaotic instincts, might even expect to gain the resurgence of those dreams and myths that the philistines have done their utmost to suppress. It is senseless to interfere, to try to avert the catastrophe; all one can do is to recoil into one's private fate. "The world is what it is and I am what I am," he declares. "I expose myself to the destructive elements that surround me. I let everything wreak its own havoc with me. I bend over to spy on the secret processes to obey rather than to command." And again: "I'm neither for nor against, I'm neutral. . . . If to live is the paramount thing, then I will live even if I become a cannibal." And even in his own proper sphere the artist is no longer free to construct objective forms. He must abandon the "literary gold standard" and devote himself to creating biographical works —human documents rather than "literature"—depicting man in the grip of delirium.

And Miller's practice fits his theory. His novels do in fact dissolve the forms and genres of writing in a stream of exhortation, narrative, world-historical criticism, prose-poetry and spontaneous philosophy, all equally subjected to the strain and grind of self-expression at all costs. So riled is his ego by external reality, so confused and helpless, that he can no longer afford the continual sacrifice of personality that the act of creation requires, he can no longer bear to express himself implicitly by means of the work of art as a whole but must simultaneously permeate and absorb each of its separate parts and details. If everything else has failed me, this author seems to say, at least this book is mine, here everything is fashioned in my own image, here I am God.

This is the meaning, I think, of the "biographical" aesthetic that Miller at once practiced and preached in his early work and which an increasing number of writers, though not cognizant of it as a program, nevertheless practice in the same compulsive manner, not necessarily for reasons as personal as Miller's or with the same results, but because the growing alienation of man in modern society throws them back into narcissistic attitudes, forces them to undertake the shattering task of possessing the world that is now full of abstractions and mystifications through the instrumentality of the self and the self alone. Not "Know Thyself!" but "Be Yourself!" is their motto. Thomas Wolfe was such a writer, and his career was frustrated by the fact that he lacked sufficient consciousness to understand his dilemma. Miller, on the other hand, was well aware of his position when writing his early fictions. Instead of attempting to recover the lost relation to the world, he accepted his alienated status as his inexorable fate, and by so doing he was able to come to some kind of terms with it.

If freedom is the recognition of necessity, then what Miller gained was the freedom to go the whole length in the subversion of values, to expose more fully perhaps than any other contemporary novelist in English the nihilism of the self which has been cut off from all social ties and released not only from any allegiance to the past but also from all commitments to the future. The peculiarly American affirmation voiced by Whitman was thus completely negated in Miller. Total negation instead of total affirmation! No wonder that like Wolfe and Hart Crane and other lost souls he was continually haunted by Whitman as by an apparition. In *Tropic of Cancer* he speaks of him as "the one lone figure which America has produced in the course of her brief life . . . the first and last poet . . . who is almost undecipherable today, a monument covered with rude hieroglyphs for which there is no key." And it is precisely because he had the temerity to go the whole length that Miller is important as a liter-

164

ary character, though his importance, as George Orwell has observed, may be more symptomatic than substantial, in the sense that the extreme of passivity, amoralism, and acceptance of evil that his novels represent tends to demonstrate "the impossibility of any major literature until the world has shaken itself into a new shape."

In all his books Miller apostrophizes the Dadaists, the Surrealists and the seekers and prophets of the "marvelous," wherever they may be found. Perhaps because he discovered the avant-gardists so late in life, he is naive enough to take their system of verbal ferocity at its face value and to adopt their self-inflationary mannerisms and outcries. At the same time he likes to associate himself with D. H. Lawrence, who was not at all an avant-gardist in the Parisian group sense of the term. He apparently regards himself as Lawrence's successor. But the truth is that they have very little in common, and there is no better way of showing it than by comparing their approaches to the sexual theme.

Miller is above all morally passive in his novels, whereas Lawrence, though he too was overwhelmed by the alienation of modern man, was sustained throughout by his supreme gift for moral activity; and he was sufficiently high-visioned to believe that a change of heart was possible, that he could reverse the current that had so long been running in one direction. Hence his idea of sexual fulfillment as a means of reintegration. Miller, however, in whose narratives sex forms the main subject-matter, presents sexual relations almost without exception in terms of fornication, which are precisely the terms that Lawrence simply loathed. The innumerable seductions, so casual and joyless, that Miller describes with such insistence on reproducing all the ribald and obscene details, are almost entirely on the level of street encounters. He has none of Molly Bloom's earthiness, nor does he ever quake with Lawrence's holy tremors. He treats erotic functions with a kind of scabrous humor, for there is scarcely any feeling in him for the sex-partner as a human being. What he wants is once and for all to expose "the conjugal orgy in the Black Hole of Calcutta." Not that he is open to the charge of pornography; on the contrary, behind his concentration on sexual experience there is a definite literary motive, or rather a double motive: first, the use of this experience to convey a sense of cultural and social disorder, to communicate a nihilist outlook, and second, an insatiable naturalistic curiosity. It is plain that Miller and Lawrence are opposites rather than twins.

Miller's claims as a guide to life and letters or as a prophet of doom can be easily discounted, though one remembers an essay by him on Proust and Joyce, called "The Universe of Death," which is a truly inspired piece of criticism. In his three novels, however, he is remarkable as the biographer of the hobo-intellectual and as the poet of those people at the bottom of society in whom some unforeseen or surreptitious contact with art and literature has aroused a latent antagonism to ordinary living, a resolve to escape the treadmill even at the cost of hunger and degradation. In dealing with this material, Miller has performed a new act of selection. There is in his fiction, also, a Dickensian strain of caricature which comes to the surface again and again, as in the riotously funny monologues of the journalists Carl and Van Norden in *Tropic of Cancer*. The truth is that his bark is worse than his bite. He strikes the attitudes of a wild man, but what he lacks is the murderous logic and purity of his European prototypes. Though he can be as ferocious as Céline, he is never so consistent; and the final impression we have of his novels is that of a naturally genial and garrulous American who has been through hell. But now that he has had a measure of recognition and has settled down at home to receive the homage of his admirers he seems to have entered a new phase, and his work only occasionally reminds us of the role of bohemian desperado which in his expatriate years he assumed with complete authority and conviction.

1940-1942

166

III. MRS. WOOLF
AND MRS. BROWN

In her wonderfully high-spirited essay "Mr. Bennett and Mrs. Brown," written in 1924, Virginia Woolf came out for scrapping the convential realism of the Edwardian generation, the generation of Wells, Galsworthy, and Bennett. The new course for English fiction, she declared, is being set by novelists like Joyce and Forster and Lawrence and herself, who were discarding the old outworn methods. Confident that they could be relied on to make good the promise of the age, she boldly predicted that it would prove to be "one of the great ages of English literature." But in conclusion she warned that it could be reached only "if we are determined never, never to desert Mrs. Brown."

Mrs. Brown, the old lady in the railway carriage, served Mrs. Woolf as the symbol of reality—of reality as we think we know it and of the human character as we live it daily and hourly. It was Mrs. Woolf's idea, in other words, that no adequate substitute for Mrs. Brown can be found but that it is possible to devise new ways of coping with the rather stodgy yet ever so obstinate old lady. Now, however, in evaluating the actual literary practice that followed and by some years even preceded the theoretical flights of her manifesto against the Edwardians, the questions that need to be asked are these: What really happened between Mrs. Woolf and Mrs. Brown? Did Mrs. Woolf succeed in holding on to Mrs. Brown or was she finally forced to desert her? And if she deserted her, as I think she did, what were the consequences of this act? Did it reduce or increase her powers as a novelist who was also one of the leading innovators in modern writing? Our judgment not only of Mrs. Woolf's fiction but of contemporary fiction in general is affected by whatever answers can be given to such questions.

E. M. Forster is among the critics who have applauded Mrs. Woolf's creative efforts; and he appears to snub Mrs. Brown when speaking of *The Waves*, surely the most abstract of Mrs. Woolf's novels, as her best work. But in another passage of the same essay he implicitly modifies his estimate of her achievement. There are two kinds of life in fiction, he observes, "life on the page and life eternal," and it is only the first kind of life that Mrs. Woolf was able to master. "Her characters never seem unreal, however slight or fantastic their lineaments, and they can be trusted to behave appropriately. Life eternal she could seldom give; she could seldom so portray a character that it was remembered afterwards on its own account." Mrs. Woolf no doubt made a very brave attempt to break through conventional realism and to create new forms for the novel. *Mrs. Dalloway* and *To the Lighthouse* are minor successes and unique in their way, but on the whole she failed. Some years ago William Troy outlined the full extent of this failure in a brilliant essay, in which he demonstrated that Mrs. Woolf's style is the product of a "facile traditionalism," that the unity of her novels is "merely superficial or decorative, corresponding to no fundamental organization of the experience," and that her characters are "unable to function anywhere but on the plane of the sensibility."

Mr. Troy's definitive analysis may be supplemented by several observations. There is the fact, for example, that at one time Mrs. Woolf thought of herself as an associate of Joyce, whereas actually there is little kinship between them. Consider to what totally different uses they put such a device as the interior monologue. While in Joyce the interior monologue is a means of bringing us closer to the characters, of telling us *more* about them than we could learn from a purely objective account of their behavior, in Mrs. Woolf it becomes a means of telling us *less* about them, of disengaging their ego from concrete situations in life and converting it into a vehicle of poetic memory. Her tendency is to drain the interior monologue of its modern content and turn it back to the habitual forms of lyrical expression—and reverie. Where Joyce performs a radically new act of aesthetic selection, Mrs. Woolf performs what is in the main an act of exclusion; for she retains no more fictional material than will suffice to identify the scene and its human inhabitants; beyond that all is sensation and impression of a volatile kind. And it is so volatile because only on the surface does it flow from the actual experience of the characters—its real source is the general tradition of English poetry and of the poetic sensibility. However, there is a crucial fault in Mrs. Woolf's grasp even of this tradition, for she comprehends it one-sidedly, and perhaps in much too feminine a fashion, not as a complete order but first and foremost as an order of sentiments.

In *Between the Acts*, Mrs. Woolf's last and most unhappy book, the following complaint is sounded time and again: "None speaks with a single voice. None with a voice free from the old vibrations. Always I hear corrupt murmurs; the chink of gold and metal. Mad music. . . ." One feels that this is the author's requiem for a lost art, that here she is pronouncing judgment against herself. But it is by no means the final judgment. Something remains that is deeply moving, an expiatory tenderness, the soul's searching of its own roots. To read her closely is to catch the strains of that "mad music" that sometimes possessed her, a music which breaks through the "old vibrations," the used-up words and disembodied imagery

169

of such "poetic" abstractions as Time and Change, Life and Death. It is the deranged song of Septimus Smith, who is Mrs. Dalloway's double and who dies that she may live. Septimus is the mysterious stranger, the marked man, the poet upon whom an outrage had been committed; he is at once the sacrificial goat and a veritable "lord of creation." This apparition haunted Mrs. Woolf, but always she strove to escape from it. She felt more at home with Mrs. Dalloway.

The ultimate failure of Virginia Woolf's experiments might perhaps be explained by going back to her initial conception of reality as an old lady in a railway carriage called Mrs. Brown. For what is Mrs. Brown if not the product of the traditional realism of the English novel? What is she if not the dominant figure of that world so scorned by Mrs. Woolf—the world of Messrs. Wells, Galsworthy, and Bennett? The truth is that she tacitly accepted, even as she revolted against her elders, their innermost vision of reality. Hence all she could do is turn their vices inside out—since they had materialized the novel she was to devote herself to spiritualizing it. Forgotten was the pledge "never, never to desert Mrs. Brown." But Mrs. Woolf was profoundly mistaken in her belief that she had seen through Mrs. Brown and was now free to dismiss her. If literature can be said to have a permanent theme, that theme is precisely The Mystery of Mrs. Brown, who is a creature of many paradoxes and truly unfathomable. She is not to be encompassed either by the materialist or by the idealist approach and she lets the novelists make what they can of her. To some she appears as a commonplace old lady; to others as a tiger in the night.

Mrs. Woolf's idea of Mrs. Brown is expressive of all the assumptions she was born to, of the safety and domestication of that upper-class British culture to which she was so perfectly adjusted. Now the breach between poetry and prose, conceived as opposed to each other in the same absolute way (but is it absolute?) that pleasure is opposed to pain, is one of the most secure assumptions of that culture; and Mrs. Woolf carried its traditional dualism to its furthest extreme. Therefore she was forced to invent a definition of what is real, of what life is, quite as artificial as the one she repudiated. "Life," she declaimed in her essay "Modern Fiction," "is not a series of gig lamps symmetrically arranged; life is a luminous halo, a semi-transparent envelope surrounding us from the beginning of consciousness to the end." That is the essence of idealism, of that other, that sacrosanct reality in which Mrs. Woolf luxuriates but from which Mrs. Brown is excluded.

Yet if Mrs. Woolf was not a great literary artist, she was surely a great woman of letters. "She liked writing," as Mr. Forster says, "with an intensity that few writers have attained, or even desired." *The Death of the Moth,* her last collection of essays and reviews, while not quite so impressive as the two volumes of *The Common Reader,* contains at least a half dozen pieces that are first rate. Never a systematic critic, she was a master of such neglected forms as the literary portrait and the familiar essay. And it is her enthusiasm and the purity and passion of her devotion to writing, rather than the poetic code which she endeavored to impose on the fictional medium, that will in the end secure a place for her, even though of the secondary order, in the history of English letters.

1942

IV. KOESTLER AND
HOMELESS RADICALISM

It is above all the quality of relevance in Arthur Koestler that makes for the lively interest in him. This quality is not to be equated with the merely topical or timely. What enters into it, chiefly, is something far more difficult to capture—a sense of the present in its essence, a sense of contemporaneity at once compelling and discriminating. It is precisely for lack of this quality that most current writing in the tradition of radical journalism is so dull and depressing, putting our intelligence to sleep with its fatal immersion in backward problems; and where the problems are politically not backward, it is usually the approach that makes them so.

Koestler, on the other hand, has taken hold with dramatic force of a large historical theme. He is at once the poet and ideologue of the homeless radical, and his unflagging analysis of this significant latter-day type—of his dilemma and pathos—has a tonic value compared to which the "positive contributions" featured in our liberal weeklies seem puerile and inane. Nothing is ultimately so enervating as unreal positiveness, whether it takes the form of the ultra-leftist's faith in the imminence of the ideal revolution or the liberal's acceptance of the Soviet myth in accordance with all the precepts of "wave of the

173

future" romanticism. Koestler, despite certain bad slips in the past, is one of the very few writers of the Left not intimidated by the demand for easy affirmations. He understands the positive function of precisely those ideas that help, in Kierkegaard's phrase, "to keep the wound of the negative open."

Koestler is, of course, neither a systematic nor an original thinker. What he exemplifies, rather, is the finest type of European journalism, whose chief advantage over the best American brand lies in its capacity to move with ease within a cultural framework (ours is more efficient in the assembly and organization of facts). Thus Koestler's prose, in which the sensibility of politics is combined with that of literature in what might be described as a psycho-political style, is far superior to anything comparable in American journalism, whether of the straight or fictional variety. Admirable, too, is Koestler's capacity to invent new terms and to order his thought in pithy formulations that sum up an entire period or the experience of an entire generation. His verbal sense is not unlike Trotsky's; the writing of both is distinguished by epigrammatic speed and wit. But Koestler is apt to sacrifice precision for the sake of startling effects or romantic contrasts. His language is occasionally too showy for comfort; and an element of the meretricious is to be detected in his all too easy use of dashingly advanced metaphors drawn from the natural sciences and the tantalizing vocabularies of the newer psychology. It might be said that in his books the phrase often goes beyond the content; that is the price he pays for his facile brilliance.

To my mind, Koestler's best work is to be found in *Spanish Testament* and *Scum of the Earth,* which are accounts of personal experience unmarred by the opportunistic turns his imagination takes when endowed with the freedom of the novelist to order his world as he pleases. For as a novelist Koestler has very little real feeling for existence as texture and pattern or for his

174

cial value of revolutionary action by attributing to it a neurotic origin. Such procedure is an obvious example of the genetic fallacy. It has likewise been said that Koestler traduces the psychoanalytic profession by depicting Sonia, its representative in the story, as an image of polymorphous sexuality and the surrender to purely instinctual life. Through this maneuver psychoanalysis is censured for its unflattering picture of human nature much in the same way that right-wing polemicists have at times gratuitously censured Marxism for the evils of the class struggle. It seems to me, however, that Koestler's attitude to Freudian ideas is not in the least hostile; and I would explain his fancy picture of Sonia by his tendency to sensationalize his material even at the cost of obscuring his meaning. This novelist is enough of a journalist not to be able to resist a scoop. Also, one should keep in mind that Sonia is cast in the role of a proponent of the nonpolitical life. Now a writer as thoroughly political as Koestler cannot but identify the nonpolitical life with a lower form of existence, that is to say, with the subhistorical. It is in this sense, I think, that we should interpret his dislike of Sonia, voiced by one of the characters who speaks of her as an "opulent Amazon" maintaining an "odious intimacy with the forbidden regions where archaic monsters dwelt. . . ."

But Koestler's treatment of the Freudian motive is not nearly so dubious as his resolution of the political problem in this novel. The problem facing his hero is that of reconciling his radical convictions with his enlistment in the British army, in the service of values gone musty, "whose force is the power of inertia." The answer given by Koestler is that even if in the dynamics of history the bourgeois democracies act not as the engine but the brake, there is real need for a brake when the engine begins running wild. This is good enough, perhaps, as a reason for a policy of strategic expediency in supporting a democratic war against totalitarianism in order to obtain a second chance for the socialist cause. There is so little

177

pathos, however, in such calculations that Koestler makes every effort to lay hold of something more profound. Hence we are told that, furthermore, "reasons do not matter," and that "he who accepts in spite of his objections . . . he will be secure." The latter argument is wholly unrelated to the first argument, and by bringing it forward the way he does Koestler appears to capitulate to the irrational drives of present-day politics. Yet even this turns out to be not sufficiently "profound," for later on it is asserted that the age of science is over and that salvation will come through a "new god" who is about to be born. Here we are finally consoled with the rhetoric of the new religiosity, whose ambition it is to replace the newly lost illusions with illusions lost long ago. If a new god is about to be born and as yet we know, as Koestler admits, neither his message nor his cult, then why not let the world go hang while we wait for this unknown god to reveal himself?

It is worth noting, however, that in *The Yogi and the Commissar,* a volume of essays brought out shortly after the appearance of *Arrival and Departure,* Koestler seems to have overcome his mystical yearnings, for here he speaks of his refusal to join the "exotic hermitage fit for Yogi exercises." The title-piece of this volume strikes me as of small consequence insofar as its key terms, Yogi amd Commissar, merely describe the polarization of belief between the concepts of change from without and change from within; and in another sense these terms come to little more than a rather sensational restatement of the old *divertissement* of the psychologists that divides all of us into introverts and extroverts. But if not meaningful in the way of uncovering a permanent human contradiction, these terms do have meaning in their application to present-day realities. For it is the vileness of what Koestler calls "Commissar-ethics," whether of the fascist or Stalinist variety, that has created the historical situation determining the movement of so many intellectuals to the ultraviolet pole of the Yogi. The Yogis in our

178

midst are continually gaining prestige and new recruits, with sorry results, however, so far as creative ideas are concerned. Auden, for instance, neglecting his splendid gifts as satirist and observer of the external world, has gone to school to Kierkegaard and Barth only to emerge as an exponent of stylized anxiety. Marx saw in the spirit of spiritless conditions the social essence of religion, and it may well be said that except for this sentiment of wretchedness the present appeal of supernaturalism has quite literally no other objective content.

What is of considerable value in Koestler's essay on the intelligentsia is the contrast drawn between the historical roles of the Russian and Western intellectuals. In the intellectuals Koestler sees a social group driven by "an aspiration to independent thought"—a group now declining in all countries, debilitated by its political experiences and gradually penned in by the growing power of the State.—"Thus the intelligentsia, once the vanguard of the ascending bourgeoisie, becomes the lumpenbourgeoisie in the age of its decay." This last seems particularly applicable to America. Not so long ago a good many of our intellectuals were economically no better off than lumpen-proletarians, a position which allowed them to assume attitudes of cultural intransigence toward society, whereas of late, what with the prosperity of the last war and the proliferation of jobs, both in the government and in educational institutions, the once impoverished intellectuals have been converted almost to a man into lumpen-bourgeois. And lumpen-bourgeois, who combine an inherent sense of insecurity with sufficient status and revenue to make them pine for more, are notoriously feeble in their aspirations to independent thought.

When it comes, however, to Koestler's imputation of neuroticism to the intelligentsia as a group, one cannot agree with him quite so easily. In his view neuroticism is the "professional disease" of the intellectuals because of the pathological pattern produced by the hostile pressure of society. Koestler may be right, but I cannot say that I

179

found his argument convincing. Precise etiological data are missing; without a controlled Freudian analysis the Freudian conclusions hang in the air; and in general the kind of observation that Koestler brings to bear is literary rather than scientific. It seems to me that he assimilates the intellectuals far too readily to the artist-types among them, who are after all but a minority within a minority. The personality structure of the artist is quite different from that of most members of the intelligentsia, whose connection is with the more technical and less estranged forms of culture and who are not noted in any special way for the vulnerability, complication or perversity of their subjective life.

Equally schematic, to my mind, are the arguments advanced in some of Koestler's essays that deal directly with literature. Thus in "The Novelist's Temptations" he makes the point that to function properly the novelist must possess "an all-embracing knowledge of the essential currents and facts (including statistics), of the ideas and theories (including the natural sciences) of his time." The saving proviso is that "this knowledge is not for actual use. . . . It is for use by implication." Even with this proviso, however, this appears to be an excessively rationalistic view of the literary process. The movements of the imagination are tortuous and obscure; great works of fiction have often been created by compulsive and extremely one-sided talents (consider the cases of Gogol or Kafka). The element of knowledge in imaginative literature is easily overestimated. What is important in writing as in art generally is the quality of relevance—a quality perhaps synonymous with that "sense of modernity" which Baudelaire stressed so frequently and for which he praised artists like Courbet and Manet. This modernity can take various and contradictory forms, some of them unrecognizable to those above all concerned with being up to date. Kafka, for instance, is deeply modern not because the latest acquisitions of the social and natural sciences are embodied in his work but because it is

180

reverberant with the feelings of loss and unreality characteristic of modern man. Being *au courant* with the latest facts and theories is desirable in itself and can certainly do the novelist a lot of good. There is no need, however, to elevate such useful knowledge to a prerequisite of the creative life.

1946

V. MELVILLE AND HIS CRITICS

Newton Arvin's *Herman Melville* is, to my mind, the finest critical biography of an American author that we have had for a long time. It is also the best book Arvin has written; he transcends in it the limitations of tone and method manifest in his works on Hawthorne and Whitman. Here he is in complete possession of his subject and uninhibited by ideological preconceptions. He treats text and context with equal authority, combining in a masterly way the traditional resources of literary criticism with a flexible and entirely apposite use of the insights provided by the newer psychological disciplines. The result is a critical interpretation so just and clear that it may well become the classic study of Melville in our literature.

Melville has of late nearly eclipsed Henry James as the much-favored object of critical inquiry. A few of the new studies devoted to him are welcome contributions to scholarship; but some of the others, in which a critical approach is attempted, are of dubious value, since what is displayed in them is less insight into Melville than an addiction to the more aberrant tendencies of the contemporary literary mind. There is the new pedantry of myth, for instance, which is well on its way to converting a valid though by no means inexhaustible cultural interest into a pretentious and up-to-date version of the kind of source-and-parallel hunting now rapidly going out of fashion in the more alert academic circles. That there is a genuine mythic element in Melville is hardly open to doubt. But the myth-happy critics blow it up to vast proportions, laboring gratuitously, and in a mode of erudition peculiarly arid, to interpose between us and the reality of Melville a talmudic elaboration of mythology portentous to the point of stupefaction.

Not quite so one-sided yet unsatisfactory on the whole is the traditionalist approach to Melville. The literary traditionalists (whose point of view is scarcely distinguishable these days from that of the "new critics") make what they can of him with their means, and their means are well adapted to eliminate the contradictions in him. But these contradictions are really of an immitigable nature. At once creative and frustrating, agonisingly personal yet deeply expressive of national and universal culture, they are at the very core of Melville's modernity and the symbolic fate of his genius. Now a Melville relieved of his contradictions is, of course, a Melville removed from the shifting and perilous terrain of history and safely committed to a transcendent realm where, ceasing to be fallible and alive, no longer desperately striving for illumination in a siege of darkness, he is canonised as an exalted witness to metaphysical faith and aesthetic order.

The traditionalist aesthetic, with its profound revulsion from historicism and psychology and its inner drive toward standards of the normative-classicist type, cannot accept the real Melville or sustain him without doing violence to itself. Hence it constructs an ideal figure who is but a ghost of the man of whom Hawthorne wrote that he could neither believe nor be comfortable in his unbelief, reasoning endlessly about "everything that lies beyond human ken" even as he despaired of immortality and "pretty much made up his mind to be annihilated."

Hawthorne, who was so frequently made inaccessible by the cold clarity of his nature, was moved by Melville's passion and believed in his integrity. None would now deny that integrity, but what is it, actually, if not the integrity of his riven and dissonant consciousness? This consciousness is inseparable from his art—an art which, in transforming the business of whaling into a fiery hunt ("wonder ye at the fiery hunt?"), makes us see the artist in the image of those sea-captains of whom he said in *Moby Dick* that though they sailed anonymously out of Nantucket they yet became "as great and greater than your Cooke and your Krusenstern, for in their succorless emptyhandedness, they, in the heathenish sharked waters, and by the beaches of unrecorded, javelin islands, battled with virgin wonders and terrors." Conrad's dictum, "In the destructive element immerse," comes to much the same thing. These "heathenish sharked waters" compose an element situated on the other side of the planet from the inland lakes of traditionalism.

Arvin, who in his present phase is perhaps freer of confining allegiances than most critics, is able to lay hold of the contradictions in Melville and to disclose their psychodynamic meaning without any squeamishness or failure in sympathy. There is no separation of man and artist in this critical portrait but an integration of the two which enforces the understanding of both in their organic unity. Eschewing all stress on biographical and historical facts for their own sake, and so controlling his account of the man Melville, of his background and character, as to enable the reader to see more clearly into his art, Arvin demonstrates anew the relevance of the biographical mode to the job of criticism when it is properly utilized and not made an end in itself. Equally credible is Arvin's use of the Freudian psychology. It is brought to bear upon Melville's experience with a maturity of judgment and power of modulation rarely found in literary contexts, where the amateurish shuffling of the formulas of neurosis is still the rule rather than the exception. In

184

spite of long and intensive discussion, the issue of psychoanalysis in its application to literature remains unsettled, arousing hostile distrust in some quarters and excessive confidence in others. From this standpoint Arvin's book might be taken as a practical experiment, offering concrete evidence which neither the friends nor the enemies of the psychoanalytic method can afford to overlook.

All of Melville's work, including the poems, is minutely examined in this study, resulting in a valuation that differs considerably from accepted judgments. Thus "Benito Cereno" is pulled down from its high place in the canon and shown to be basically lacking in the imaginative quality conventionally attributed to it. "An artistic miscarriage, with moments of undeniable power," Arvin calls it in a passage of exhaustive analysis, which lays bare the story's defective moral structure as well as the relative poverty of its technical devices and verbal texture. In his judgment of *The Confidence Man,* however, Arvin restores the negative estimate of it commonly accepted until it was recently challenged by an ambitious ideological approach which put a load of interpretation upon the book which it cannot carry.

The Confidence Man is a narrative which Arvin finds even more disappointing than *Israel Potter,* and that precisely because its "ideal" intention is such that had it been realized it might have become a "vaster, more animated, and of course more modern *Ship of Fools,* or even an American *Gulliver."* There is a wonderful felicity in the Western river-scene that Melville conceived for it and the richest meaning in its theme, the exposure of "contemporary shams, and particularly the quackeries of a false humanitarianism, an insensate optimism." This, in fact, was the most pertinent of all subjects in Melville's age. But *The Confidence Man* was never really written. It is a worse book than *Pierre,* I think. Though *Pierre* is a failure, and even a failure of a peculiarly monstrous kind, it still exercises a certain appeal, a certain power of

185

evocation, because it is full of passion and swarms with unconscious life. Not so *The Confidence Man*, which, except for its opening pages, strictly enforces the lesson that in art nothing speaks to our mind which does not simultaneously engage our senses: that is the supreme lesson, and one which criticism fails to heed only at the risk of utter irrelevance. And the reason, obviously, that this disputed work of Melville's remains, as Arvin says, "a tantalizing scenario for a book that never came into being," is that it is scarcely at all a living narrative. "One is alleged to be on a steamboat descending the greatest of American rivers, but sensuously, pictorially, kinesthetically . . . the river does not flow and the boat does not move ahead." As a fiction the book is "meager and monotonous . . . all but motionless . . . a series of conversations rather than an action . . . which keep recurring to the same theme too compulsively, with too few variations, to be anything but unendurably repetitious." Arvin pursues his analysis to the ultimate conclusion that this work is "one of the most completely nihilistic, morally and metaphysically," of American books, suffering from a "fatal want of moral chiaroscuro," Melville's *Timon of Athens* without a Flavius. Its actual effect is more of tameness than of terror, since what "it expresses, except at rare moments, is not a passion of bitterness but a dull despondency of mistrust and disbelief." Melville wrote it in a state of morbid suspiciousness when he had lost the vision of tragic grandeur that makes *Moby Dick* the chief masterpiece of American letters.

The most richly assimilative of his critical tasks Arvin undertakes in his comprehensive scrutiny of that masterpiece. Varied resources of literary and philosophical investigation are pressed into service in an unflagging effort to grasp, to understand, to bring to light. The analysis is conducted on the four levels of the literal, the psychological, the moral, and the mythic; and it is so comprehensive an analysis that it would be impossible to do it justice in a brief résumé. Suffice it to say that it

186

yields a reading of *Moby Dick* summing up the best that we have learned about it at the same time that it establishes some wholly new relations of meaning and a sharper perception of the coherence of its parts in the unity of imaginative possession.

The Shakespearean influence on Melville has been sufficiently charted by scholars like Olson and Matthiessen, and on that score Arvin has little to add that is newly suggestive. Of more original value is his examination of Melville's problem in seeking to discover the proper form for his narratives. Melville was working in isolation from the central currents of European writings, an isolation from which he both lost and gained. As *Pierre* shows, he foundered in attempting to adopt as his own the typical novelistic forms developed by his contemporaries in Europe. This problem and the fashion in which Melville proceeded to solve it are of far more than technical importance. We are confronted here with an aspect of the national literary experience that indirectly but significantly connects certain elementary considerations of manner and technique with the higher considerations of form and value.

1950

VI. HEMINGWAY IN THE 1950'S

The first thing to be remarked about *Across the River and into the Trees* is that it is so egregiously bad as to render all comment on it positively embarrassing to anyone who esteems Hemingway as one of the more considerable prose-artists of our time and as the author of some of the finest short stories in the language. Hence the disappointment induced by this latest work of his, a work manifestly composed in a state of distemper, if not actual demoralization.

This novel reads like a parody by the author of his own manner—a parody so biting that it virtually destroys the mixed social and literary legend of Hemingway that has now endured for nearly three decades. For it can be said that not since the days of Dickens and later of Mark Twain has a writer of fiction in English succeeded in beguiling and captivating his readers to the extent that Hemingway did; and his success had a quality of ease and naturalness that was essentially exhilarating. In this latest book, however, the legend suffers irremediable damage. Here he really goes too far in the exploitation of it, indulging himself in blatant self-pity and equally blatant conceit, with the result that certain faults of personality, and the moral and intellectual immaturity which he was

188

never able to overcome but which heretofore, in the greater part of his creative work, he managed to sublimate with genuine artistry, now come through as ruling elements, forcing the reader to react to Hemingway the man rather than to Hemingway the artist. And the man in Hemingway—in his literary appearances at any rate —has nearly always struck one as the parasitical double of the artist in him.

This cleavage between man and artist was long ago perceived by his more acute critics. Thus Edmund Wilson observed that "something frightful seems to happen to Hemingway as soon as he begins to write in his own person. In his fiction, the conflicting elements of his personality, the emotional situations that obsess him, are externalized and objectified; and the result is an art which is severe, intense, and deeply serious. But as soon as he talks in his own person he seems to lose all his capacity for self-criticism and is likely to become fatuous or maudlin." Now though this new narrative is written not in the first person but in the fictional third person, still it is precisely the element of the fatuous and the maudlin that predominates in it. The explanation for that lies, I think, in the insecure division between man and artist in Hemingway. The strain of sustaining it has been obviously getting him down and the artist has been gradually giving way to the man.

That this was the case was already becoming apparent in sections of *To Have and Have Not,* a poor novel on the whole, whose protagonist, Harry Morgan, was presented, in a manner unmistakably and disagreeably subjective, as a kind of totem of sexual virility. The infantile nature of the fantasy was plain and so was the subliterary effect. Then one came upon the same sort of thing in parts of *For Whom the Bell Tolls,* particularly in the parts celebrating the love-making of Robert Jordan and Maria; and in *Across the River and into the Trees* the personal brag and splutter is even more jarring, for here the artist appears to have been entirely displaced by the man. In fact there is hardly any aesthetic distance between the author and Colonel Richard Cantwell, the hero of the novel. They have so much in common, in their private history and war experience no less than in their opinions, tastes, attitudes, and prejudices, that there is no telling them apart. Thus the author intrudes everywhere, violating the most elementary specifications making for verisimilitude in a work of fiction. For example, why is this colonel of the regular U.S. Army, who on the face of it is no great shakes as a worldly character, treated in the luxurious Venice hotels and bars with the minute deference usually reserved for the celebrities of international café society? As for the obsessive consumption of food and liquor, especially liquor, and the pride taken in the knowledge and selection of them, that certainly belongs to the more recent versions of the Hemingway legend; but it is wholly unconvincing as an integral part of the characterization of an army officer of the type of Colonel Cantwell. Though these may be small details they point to an identification of author and hero disruptive of the primary and indispensable aesthetic illusion.

The time span of the story is three days, the scene is Venice and the Adriatic countryside, and the action consists of a duck shoot, which is far and away the best bit in the book, and, for the rest, of prolonged love passages between the Colonel and his girl, the nineteen-year-old Countess Renata, who is not a recognizable human being at all but a narcissistically constructed love-object. She is even less credible than Maria of the Spanish novel. Both belong to the tradition of adoring and submissive Hemingway girls, a type that has been getting more and more adoring and submissive as the years pass. Renata, the latest incarnation, is surely the most unreal of the lot, wholly the product of an adolescent revery of irresistible mastery and perfection of experience in love. The ritualistic love-talk between the Colonel and this girl is of an indescribable tediousness, and the way in which he introduces his war memories into the talk is structurally so artificial as to deprive the recalled experience of the authority it implicitly lays claim to. The war scenes evoked in this book come off very badly in comparison with the actual representation of war in *A Farewell to Arms* and *For Whom the Bell Tolls*. What is missing here is "the real thing, the sequence of motion and fact which made the emotion," as Hemingway once put it with the precision of a conscientious artist speaking of his craft.

The stated themes of love and death are unrealized in this novel. The Colonel dies of heart disease as the action ends, but we are prepared for his death only factually, not imaginatively. It is an occurrence, nothing more, devoid of expressive implications, since the story turns on no significant principle of honor or valor or compassion such as invested some of Hemingway's earlier narratives with value and meaning. This could not but happen once the author became involved with his hero in exactly the wrong way, shifting from the role of creator to that of devotee pure and simple. He is unaware, or only dimly aware, of his hero's vanity and brutality and of the ugly competitiveness exhibited in his relations to other human beings. There can be no evaluation of character or behavior in such a contest, and no intelligible meaning to the action.

It is true, of course, that Hemingway has always been more closely involved with his hero than most novelists. The relation in which he stood to him, however, was not that of literal and helpless identification but that of the ego to the ego-ideal. Seeking to "find himself" in this leading character, he endowed him with all the qualities he considered admirable; and the world into which he turned him loose to do or die, though real enough, was none the less specially selected and ordered so as to provide him with the conditions he needed for self-fulfillment. These were conditions of relative freedom from normal circumstances and routine compulsions, for it is only within the special ambience of combat and virile sports that he performed his part, discovering the fate that

191

awaited him. It seems to me that a good many qualities of Hemingway's prose are accounted for by this disengagement of his hero and his typical situation from the thick coils of environment, from its confusion of objects and facts. It certainly helped Hemingway to form a style of unusual lightness and freshness, but it did not make him a novelist of the first rank.

There is a certain kind of freedom which the greater novelists can neither afford nor care to solicit. Still, the fact that the binding agent of Hemingway's work was the personality of the hero, who alone held sway and in whom all the compositional elements were merged, made for a unity and concreteness of effect matched by very few of his contemporaries. But within this creative process there always lurked the danger of a possible merger between ego and ego-ideal that would disrupt the delicate balance allowing the author to live through his leading character imaginatively while standing apart from him as a man. That this balance has been lost is now evident. Colonel Cantwell is not Hemingway's ego-ideal, like Jake Barnes and Lieutenant Henry: he is the ego-ideal taken as achieved and absorbed into the ego of Hemingway, who is thus turned into his own complete ego-ideal. It is greatly to be hoped that in his future work the man recedes as the artist regains control.

1950

Hemingway's new story happily demonstrates his recovery from the distemper that so plainly marked his last novel, *Across the River and into the Trees*. In *The Old Man and the Sea* the artist in him appears to have recouped some of his losses, curbing the overassertive ego so easily disposed to fall into a kind of morbid irritability of self-love mixed with self-pity. It is to be hoped that the recovery is more than temporary.

But free as this latest work is of the faults of the preceding one, it is still by no means the masterpiece which

192

the nationwide publicity set off by its publication in *Life* magazine has made it out to be. Publicity is the reward as well as the nemesis of celebrities, but it has nothing in common with judgment. Though the merit of this new story is incontestable, so are its limitations. I do not believe that it will eventually be placed among Hemingway's major writings.

Moreover, it is in no sense a novel, as the publishers would have us believe. At its core it is actually little more than a fishing anecdote, though one invested with an heroic appeal by the writer's art, which here again confirms its natural affinity with the theme of combat and virile sports. This art is at its best in the supple and exact rendering of the sensory detail called for by its chosen theme; and in telling of the old fisherman's ordeal on the open sea—of his strenuous encounter with a giant marlin, the capture of him after a two-day struggle, and the loss of the carcass to the sharks in the end—Hemingway makes the most of his gifts, turning to good account the values of courage and endurance and discipline in action on which his ethic as an artist depends.

The premise of the story—its moral premise at any rate —is the purity and goodness and bravery of Santiago, the Cuban fisherman. And given Hemingway's habitual attitude of toughness coupled with sentimentality, one can easily make out the chief threat to the integrity of the writing; and it is in fact to the circumvention of sentimentality that the story owes its success. The two scenes (in which the boy displays his adoration of Santiago) that are not quite exempt from the charge of sentimentality are but indirectly related to the action. They form a lyrical prelude and postlude to the action, which is presented in fictional terms that are hard and clear. And it is saved from false sentiment by Hemingway's wonderful feeling for the sea and its creatures—a feeling that he is able to objectify with as much care and devotion as he lavishes on the old man. This creates the rare effect of our perceiving the old man and the fish he catches as if they

193

existed, like a savage and his totem, within the same psychic continuum. No wonder that at the height of his battle with the fish Santiago exclaims: "You are killing me, fish. . . . But you have a right to. Never have I seen a greater, or more beautiful, or a calmer or more noble thing than you, brother. Come on and kill me. I do not care who kills who."

When all this has been said, however, one is still left with the impression that the creative appeal of this narrative is forceful yet restricted, its quality of emotion genuine but so elemental in its totality as to exact nothing from us beyond instant assent. It exhibits the credentials of the authentic, but in itself it promises very little by way of an advance beyond the positions already won in the earlier phases of Hemingway's career. To be sure, if one is to judge by what some of the reviewers have been saying and by the talk heard among literary people, the meaning of *The Old Man and the Sea* is to be sought in its deep symbolism. It may be that the symbolism is really there, though I for one have been unable to locate it. I suspect that here again the characteristic attempt of the present literary period is being made to overcome the reality of the felt experience of art by converting it to some moral or spiritual platitude. It goes without saying that the platitude is invariably sublimated through the newly modish terms of myth and symbolism. As Lionel Trilling reported in a recent essay, students have now acquired "a trick of speaking of money in Dostoevsky's novels as 'symbolic,' as if no one ever needed, or spent, or gambled, or squandered the stuff—and as if to think of it as an actuality were sub-literary." Perhaps this latter-day tendency accounts for the inflationary readings that Hemingway's story has received, readings that typically stress some kind of schematism of spirit at the expense of the action so lucidly represented in its pages. Hemingway's big marlin is no Moby Dick, and his fisherman is not Captain Ahab nor was meant to be. It is enough praise to say that their existence is real, and that their encounter is de-

194

scribed in a language at once relaxed and disciplined which is a source of pleasure. In art, as Wallace Stevens once put it, "Description is revelation. It is not / The thing described, nor false facsimile." And I would suggest to the ingenious interpreters that they look to the denotations of a work of literature before taking off into the empyrean of pure connotation.

1952

VII. T. S. ELIOT: THE POET
AS PLAYWRIGHT

The subject of poetic drama has been for some thirty odd years now among T. S. Eliot's most enduring interests. It has preoccupied him in his capacity both as practitioner and critic, and in his latest essay, "Poetry and Drama," comprising the text of the first Theodore Spencer Memorial Lecture delivered at Harvard, he proceeds to sum up, with his usual precision and with a fine candor so surprising as to be anything but usual, what the experience of his self-education as a poet "trying to write for the theater" has come to so far.

It is a lively summing-up, engrossing in its general formulations and even more so in its author's extended comment on his own experiments in verse drama, their "intentions, failures and practical successes." This comment, admirably concrete and sensible, and all in all an unequalled feat of self-criticism, ought to confound the swarming idolizers and cultists of Eliot among the younger academic *literati* of reactionary allegiance, the *nouveaux* "new critics" as someone has aptly called them, whose habit it is to extol every new opus of their master regardless of its specific value in relation to his work as a whole. The ponderous exegeses of *The Cocktail Party* that have appeared during the past year in some of the

literary quarterlies—exegeses marked by a maximum of un-
reliable assumption and a minimum of relevant evaluation—are the latest and more egregious products of this
sterile and fatuous cultism. Now when Eliot informs us
that it is "an open question" whether there is any poetry
in that play at all, and when he puts his finger on the
chief structural defect of the play in remarking that its
third act is more in the nature of an epilogue than a true
dramatic resolution of the action, one wonders how it is
that the eager-beaver exegetes failed to notice anything of
the sort. The faults Eliot notes are hardly of an esoteric
nature, and they relate solely to the form of the play. I
think that it has other faults, too, bearing upon its basic
meaning and conception, that are perhaps undiscerned by
the author and that are equally lost on the cult-ridden
commentators.

I doubt that these people are in a position to learn anything really essential from their master. They have by now
converted Eliot into a vested interest, fastening upon the
worst side of him, his bent toward scholasticism in matters
of belief and partly in matters of art too, thus erecting a
traditionalist aesthetic which has of late grown into a
barrier to the renewal of the creative impulse in American
letters; and this they have done mostly on the strength of
Eliot's eminence as an example. What is objectionable is
the stupefying one-sidedness of their citations of this example. If one thing is certain, it is that Eliot could with
justice disclaim the image of himself presented by his
disciples. Marx once declared that he was no Marxist, and
Eliot may soon be forced to resign from the school of
Eliot. For the truth is that his contribution to the practice of modern poetry and criticism is by no means exhausted by his traditionalist bias. In the future it will be
seen, I believe, that the link between him and his disciples was forged by the *Zeitgeist* rather than by what is
most real in his achievement. The disciples dote on his
dogmatic ideology, turning it into a proof of impeccable
literary virtue, at the same time that with singular regu-

larity they shy away from recognizing the empirical genius displayed in his best insights into the creative process.

It is instructive to compare what Eliot now says about poetic drama with his remarks in the "Dialogue on Dramatic Poetry," which dates back to 1928. It is the change of tone which is above all noticeable. The "Dialogue" is full of arrogant pronouncements and the tone is combative throughout, reflecting the exasperation of a poet straining to repel the apparently irresistible encroachments of the prose medium on the drama, which he is opinionated enough to regard as belonging peculiarly to the domain of poetry. In this latest stocktaking, however, there is no longer any question of cavalierly dismissing the play in prose as a mere "by-product" of the play in verse; nor is there any trace left of such grotesque opinions as that ranking Tourneur above Ibsen as a dramatist. The current word as to Ibsen is "a great prose dramatist." Thus many years of trying to adapt versification and idiom to the needs of a modern dramatic poetry, a poetry so flexible as to be able to deal with the most matter-of-fact things no less than with the most exalted, have taught Eliot that poetic drama can be restored only if it is willing to enter into "overt competition" with prose. The easy victory scored ever prose in the "dialogue" is now implicitly seen as the illusion typical of the poet venturing into the theater with insufficient appreciation of dramatic technique.

The conclusions Eliot comes to are, firstly, that no play should be written in verse for which prose is dramatically adequate; and, secondly, that the play, whether in prose or verse, should be so absorbing to the audience that the effect of style and rhythm would prove to be nearly "unconscious." In other words, what Eliot now calls for is a more complete fusion of action and speech—a fusion helping to overcome the resistance both of those listeners who dislike poetry altogether and those who like it so much they are prepared to abstract the poetry from the play in order to enjoy it in splendid isolation as it were.

198

Hence it will not do to employ poetry in a play merely as a means of formalizing or decorating speech. Poetry in dramatic form is unjustified if "it merely gives people of literary tastes the pleasure of listening to poetry at the same time that they are witnessing a play." For then the poetry becomes superfluous, and perhaps even harmful, in that it tends to reinforce the habit of taking poetry as the speech of an unreal world.

Eliot is nothing if not intent on coping with what Henry James once called "the beautiful difficulties of art"; and, in the case of poetic drama, the difficulty which now appears to him to be most patently and stubbornly there is that of retaining the poetry while so subordinating its immediate effect as to make its integration into a dramatic whole possible. I have heard poets express suspicion of this notion, which they somehow associate with a "reductive" attitude toward their medium. Yet what Eliot is saying here is actually no more than what Keats said in his statement that "poetry should be great and unobtrusive, a thing which enters into one's soul, and does not startle or amaze with itself but with its subject." And it is because of this new conviction of the necessity of unobtrusiveness that Eliot now renounces the use of choral verse in drama. The chorus is seen as anachronistic in essence, leading nowhere so far as a general solution of the problem of poetic drama is concerned. After all, it is much easier for a poet to write choral verse than to master dramatic dialogue. The chorus was no doubt appropriately placed in a ritual play like *Murder in the Cathedral,* but in a normal dramatic context it inevitably tends to interrupt rather than to intensify the action.

In the main, the lesson that Eliot draws from his continual experimentation is that the writing of verse for a play must be approached in an entirely different frame of mind from the writing of other verse. Ordinarily a poem is written "in terms of one's own voice," and it is addressed, initially at least, to a narrow circle of readers disposed not only to receive the poet's communication favorably but to study and meditate upon it. In the verse play, on the other hand, every line "must be judged by a new law, that of dramatic relevance." One might have thought that this elementary law, with which every middling Broadway craftsman is thoroughly familiar, would have been apparent to Eliot at the very start of his experiments. But no, as is shown by his present declaration and by the evidence of *The Family Reunion,* which contains not a few passages that are dramatically irrelevant and dispersive in effect, it has taken him years of constant application to acquire a working knowledge of that law. It is true, of course, that at least for two centuries now English poets, attempting to reinstate verse as a language of the theater, have been confronted with enormous difficulties in adjusting metric and idiom to a living and natural speech-tone; it is for that reason perhaps that they have tended to make far too little of the problems of characterization and plot—and plot, in the Aristotelian sense of it as an action that is "serious and complete," is the very soul of drama.

I must confess that Eliot's latest audit of his experience in writing for the theater has made me more skeptical than ever of the ability of poets to master dramatic form while maintaining a high level of poetic expression incorporating the movements of modern speech. *The Cocktail Party* is a case in point. Here Eliot, following the "ascetic rule" of avoiding lines of verse without dramatic utility, has produced a poetry so "unobtrusive" as to be virtually nonexistent. Thus what he gains in theatrical technique he loses in poetic power. The plain conclusion is that the play might as well have been written in prose.

Also, it seems to me that *The Cocktail Party* is so deficient in plot and characterization as to merit not at all the encomiums that greeted its production on Broadway. There is a discord between the convention of drawing-room comedy it employs and its deeper aim, which is nothing less than that of getting at the essence of the human situation. What the audience warms up to is the familiar trappings of comedy; but the deeper meaning, since it remains dramatically unrealized, is impressed upon it, if at all, with the shallowness of a pious lesson or message—the price paid for the evening's diversion. For in its aspiration to get at the human essence, the play falls short as lamentably in its way as did the plays of the German Expressionists, upon whose failure the philosopher George Simmel once commented with great astuteness that they "attempt to seize life in its essence but without its content." And in its dramatic structure *The Cocktail Party* is indeed the epitome of essence without content.

The two ways of life—that of resigned mediocrity on the one hand and saintliness on the other—are expatiated upon by the playwright through his mouthpiece Harcourt-Reilly, but are so inadequately embodied in a living action that what comes through to us is no more than another theory of human existence rather than a lively representation of it. The Chamberlaynes are a couple without any life of their own; they have no motive-power except that of illustrating as neatly as possible the *Weltanschauung* which the author imposes upon them by main force. And what is one to make of Celia Coplestone, the exemplar of the second, that is, the saintly way? What can be more hollow than this attempt to enforce the claims of transcendent goodness by releasing the claimant from her dramatic obligations, so to speak, and packing her off to Africa to perform missionary work and die the death of a Christian martyr? It is too easy, too pat. The portrayal of goodness is among the most difficult tasks that any writer can undertake. Dostoevsky said many incisive things about the problem of portraying "a positively good man" in literature, and surely he would have failed utterly if in *The Idiot* he had removed Myshkin from the net of human relationships in which he becomes involved in order to transport him to some other realm, conveniently free from the pressure of such demonic beings as Rogozhin and Nastasya Filipovna, where he could perform the deeds traditionally associated in devotional writings with the Christian character assigned to him by the author. To substantiate Celia's choice of the "second way" by immersing her in the experience of modern London is one thing; to send her off to Africa to be crucified is something else again. It is religious melodrama of an appallingly conventional sort. For in the context of Eliot's play, Africa is not a real place but the domain of abstraction pure and simple. And there are other things in the play, such as the psychiatric masquerade of the clerical Sir Harcourt-Reilly, which are equally bad. Nor does it help us to appreciate the play any better when Eliot now tells us that its point of departure is the *Alcestis* of Euripides. Only the cult-ridden exegetes will take seriously the intellectual "conceit" of treating "one-eyed" Reilly as the mythic offspring of Heracles and identifying Lavinia, the woman whom no one can love, with the lost and recovered wife of Admetus. Neither by way of contrast nor similarity is this mythic correlation very interesting or revealing.

We are fortunate to have Eliot's account of his self-education as a playwright. It is a scrupulous account, convincing us of the positive nature of his effort to restore poetic drama. The effort is its own justification even if at times the result strikes one as wide of the mark.

1951

VIII. GOGOL AS A
MODERN INSTANCE*

In reflecting about Gogol while preparing my remarks for this commemorative occasion I found myself thinking of him first of all as a peculiarly modern instance of the literary artist. This may surprise those who see him entirely in terms of the Russian background, placing him all too securely within a nearly self-sufficient national tradition. There is no denying, to be sure, that the Russian background is of primary importance for the understanding of Gogol's creative course. He crosses the frontiers of language far less easily than writers like Turgenev and Dostoevsky and Tolstoy and Chekhov, whose creations exercise an appeal unconfined by differences of nationality and cultural setting. Gogol's work, with the possible exception of his story "The Overcoat," cannot be said to have become an intimate possession of the Western world; only in the Russian milieu is it an indispensable part of a literary education. But the reason for that is quite simple. Gogol's characters, like Chichikov and Khlestakov, are no less universal than the characters of Tolstoy and Dostoevsky. What hinders us in our

* Text of a talk at a public meeting in Columbia University commemorating the one-hundredth anniversary of Gogol's death.

appropriation of them is the fact that Gogol is so great a master of style and verbal orchestration that his power to move us is virtually indissoluble from his language.

Another approach to Gogol is by way of his creative psychology, in which one recognizes certain traits that recall us to the fate of modern literature. It is above all our sense of the deeply problematic character of this literature that impels us to conceive of Gogol as our contemporary. His creative psychology is so tortuous and obsessive, so given over to moods of self-estrangement and self-loathing, so marked by abrupt turns from levity to despair, that one cannot but see it as a tissue of contradictions from top to bottom. These contradictions are at once the secret of his poetic power and the cause of his ruin as a man—his tragic renunciation of the creative life in mid-career and the frightful end that came to him under the stress of a spiritual crisis of a surpassingly primitive and even savage nature. It is easy enough to expatiate on the neurotic components in his make-up, or, to put it more precisely, on the unmistakable pathology of his life-experience. Let us keep in mind, however, that in the case of great artists neuroticism is never in itself a sufficient explanation. For the neuroticism of such artists tends to assume a symbolic meaning, taking on the supra-personal significance of a general state of mind or of a radical change in consciousness. In this sense it becomes possible to relate the discontinuities and discords in Gogol to the problematical character of the modern artist as a type. Gogol's dilemma was that he was incapable of reconciling the meaning of his art with the meaning of his life. This discord, to which the artists of the modern epoch are peculiarly open, was scarcely operative in the classic ages of literature when life and art were not at war with each other but were integrated by common presuppositions and a common faith.

The problem of the separation of art and life has an objective historical import that is not to be grasped if analyzed solely from the standpoint of the artist's personal character and disposition. It is exactly from this point of view that Arnold Hauser discusses the struggles and sufferings of Flaubert. Hauser attributes Flaubert's lack of a direct relationship to life, his dogmatic aestheticism and his turning away with disdain from human existence as a symptom of "the gulf that has opened up in the modern artistic career between the possession of life and the expression of it." Gogol, too, wanted to possess his life in a manner quite incompatible with his expression of it; and there is still another way in which we might link these two novelists in spite of the obvious differences between them. Both are leading protagonists in the extremely complex and perilous passage of European literature from romanticism to realism. Like Flaubert, Gogol is an inverted Romantic trying to resolve the tension between actuality and romance, between the deflation and inflation of life's vital illusions, by the most rigorous application of rhetorical and stylistic force, by exploiting the necromantic properties of language so as to establish some kind of psychic control and a measure of moral poise, however precarious. In wholly different ways both of these literary artists used language as a shield against chaos and as a therapeutic resource; and both were compelled to create prodigious images of negation even as they inwardly yearned to utter the saving, the positive, the loving word. Thus Flaubert, who began as a Romantic, was inclined from the outset to idealize love; yet what he actually wrote is novels about the destructive effects of love and its power to entangle us in fatal illusions. The theme of love was of course closed to Gogol by his prohibitive fear of sexuality, but in his own chosen themes he too was compulsively driven to expose precisely that which he would have liked to portray in glowing colors. Starting from the invulnerably naive premise that it was his task to idealize the feudal-bureaucratic order of imperial Russia and to paint an idyllic picture of the rural squires, what he in fact produced is a picture so grotesquely satiric that it could easily be made to serve as an instrument of social disruption. Flaubert found his ideal enemy in the bourgeois, whom he tirelessly berated, while Gogol, inasmuch as in his time the Russian bourgeois existed as no more than an embryo in the body politic, seized on the government official and on the parasitic landlord as types whom he could paralyze with his satiric virus and then fix forever in the monstrous tableau his imagination constructed. Even Flaubert's statement, *Madame Bovary, c'est moi,* has its parallel in Gogol's remark that in laughing at his characters the reader was really laughing at their author, for he had impregnated them with his own looseness and "nastiness."

It is not difficult to recognize in Gogol some of the features of Dostoevsky's underground man, in particular the split between sickly, spiteful vanity on the one hand and aspirations toward truth and goodness on the other. Some Russian scholars have surmised that Dostoevsky had Gogol in mind in his portrayal of Foma Fomich, the buffoon-like protagonist of his long story "The Friend of the Family." Whether this surmise is correct or not, there is indeed something in Foma Fomich's insufferably didactic tone, in his outrageous preaching of virtue and uplift that reminds us irresistibly of Gogol's vainglorious and clownish bombast in that incredible book, *Selected Passages from the Correspondence with Friends,* probably the most implausible work ever produced by a writer of genius.

The truth is that Gogol was quite aware of his own "underground" traits, and he spoke more than once of "the terrible mixture of contradictions" of which his nature was composed. This master of language, the first truly important artist of Russian prose, strove with might and main to overcome what he regarded as the morbid negativism of his relationship to life, a striving pitiful in its futility; for as he himself admitted in "The Author's Confession," his real predilection was "for bringing out the trivialities of life, describing the vulgarity of mediocrity . . . and all those small things which generally remain unobserved." What is missing, however, in this self-analysis of Gogol's is any hint of the astonishing comic sense that enabled him to invest mediocrity and smallness of soul with a superreal quality that ultimately acts to liberate us and restore us to our humanity. The one thing that Gogol failed to believe in is that laughter cures. His conviction of guilt and unworthiness forced him to hold out obstinately against that catharsis of laughter for which his readers are immensely grateful to him.

Gogol was in no sense a cultivated man of letters. He appeared on the literary scene like an utterly unexpected and rude guest after whose departure life at home could never again be the same. It does not matter that the rude guest's performance was not quite understood for what it was, that a critic like Belinsky, for instance, could cite this performance as an overriding example of the writer's assumption of responsibility to society, of his civic consciousness and fidelity to the factually real. What was then chiefly overlooked in Gogol was the fantastic gratuity of his humor and his transcendence of the limited social motive through the unearthly and well-nigh metaphysical pathos of a supreme creation like "The Overcoat." For in truth Baschmatskin, the little copying clerk who is the hero of that story, attains a stature far greater than that of any mere victim of an unjust social system. He is a timeless apparition of humanity *in extremis,* of man homeless not only in his society but in the universe. There is one story in American literature, Melville's "Bartelby the Scrivener," which has a spiritual affinity with "The Overcoat." But it is no more than affinity. Melville's story, for all its profound overtones, lacks the inner coherence, the resonance, and marvelous stylization of Gogol's masterpiece.

But having allowed for the period prejudices of a critic like Belinsky and discounted the narrowly sociological approach to Gogol, I still cannot accept the aesthetic-modernist reading of his work that we get in Vladimir Nabokov's critical study of him. Brilliantly appreciative as Nabokov is of the grotesque side of Gogol and, indeed, of all that side of him relating to the poetry of the irrational and the spirit of incongruity and mystification, he has no eye whatever for his subject's place in literary history and social and national peculiarities. Nabokov seems to suffer from something like a phobic fear of all interpretive techniques not strictly literary in reference—a fear driving him toward the extremely one-sided emphasis which takes the literary act to be a phenomenon solely "of language and not of ideas." And Nabokov reduces his formalist bias to sheer absurdity when he goes so far as to state that "Gogol's heroes happen to be Russian squires and officials; their imagined surroundings and social conditions are perfectly unimportant." He is equally vehement in denying that Gogol can in any way be characterized as a realist. It is true, of course, that Gogol never deliberately set out to describe his social environment; but the fact is that his subjective method of exaggeration, of caricature and farce, produced an imagery of sloth, ugliness, and self-satisfied inferiority which, if not directly reflective, is none the less fully expressive of the realities of life in Czarist Russia. Moreover, Nabokov ignores the dynamic plebeianism of Gogol's genius. For that is what enabled him to make a radically new selection of material and to assimilate to his medium elements of everyday existence, with their lowlife and vulgar details, heretofore excluded by the aristocratic conventions of literature in Russia as elsewhere. Even if the creatures of his imagination are not so much "real people" as caricatures, he none the less contributed greatly to the development of realism by opening up the lower reaches and underside of life to literary portraiture.

It is impossible to abstract Gogol from his historical moment and to dissociate the necessary and contingent elements of his creative personality so as to arrive at the pure substance of Gogolism. Nabokov's rite of purification converts Gogol into the ghost of his own work. I do not object to Nabokov's Gogol because he bears so little resemblance to the Gogol of Belinksy and Dobroluibov but rather because Nabokov's Gogol is too pure to be true, too literary and abstract to be genuine. The poet who inserted into *Dead Souls* epic apostrophes to Holy Russia—apostrophes infused with messianic hope in which love and despair are inextricably mingled—was not a purist writing in a vein of exclusive subjectivity and dedicated to the tormenting refinements of his solitary dreams. He too, like all of Russia's great writers, suffered with his country and its people.

1952

IX. ART AND THE
"SIXTH SENSE"

Arnold Hauser's *Social History of Art* is concerned with literary as much as with pictorial art. Its insights into the creative process are provocative and its ideas of a more general nature are brilliantly developed. It is a work remarkable above all for its intellectual energy.

Remarkable, too, is the fact that the method deployed in it is basically that of Marxism, though not of the type we have become accustomed to and against which we have so strongly reacted in the recent past. Purged of crudities and stultifying obligations to a party line, what Mr. Hauser's Marxist bias really comes to is a kind of radical historicism which has nothing in common with the shifty and specious ideology manipulated by the culture-commissars. Yet even so Mr. Hauser's merit as critic and historian will doubtless be excessively resisted among us. The current dogma has it that radicalism, in all the diversity of its possible revisions, combinations, and permutations, is played out for good and nothing more can be said for it. This dogma I take to be a falsification committed by the *Zeitgeist,* essentially as groundless as the dogma prevailing in the thirties that assigned to radicalism a monopoly of critical thought. The abrupt swings of consciousness from one demoralizing extreme to the other that we have experienced of late are typically of our time and belong to its intellectual pathology.

As for Mr. Hauser's political attitude, to judge by the skittishness of his references to the censorship of the arts in the Soviet empire, he is far from prepared to believe the worst. Still, it would ill become us to emulate the party-line strategy of examining books strictly in terms of their authors' political opinions of the moment rather than in the light of their stated intention and inherent value. What counts for us, chiefly, is the writer's handling of his subject and the return it yields for our mental loss or gain—and Mr. Hauser's subject is not the present world situation but the social and historical background of the arts beginning with the magical drawings of the Old Stone Age (p. 23ff.) and ending with the emergence of the film as a powerful new medium and the impact of the democratization of culture in the twentieth century (p. 958).

Since the vastness of Mr. Hauser's undertaking has imposed a rigorous selectivity, our consideration of it must of necessity also be highly selective. One can hope to discuss only some aspects of the work he has produced. The particulars of his approach to painting I shall leave to the critics in that field, making what I can of his interpretation of literary figures and movements, his general method, and a few of the leading ideas he has put to use in integrating his material.

For Mr. Hauser the key word is "history" not because he is literally engaged in writing a history of art but rather because in his view the modern conception of history is the heuristic principle *par excellence*. This puts him into the camp of the historicists, to be sure, but scarcely into the camp of the academic practitioners of the "historical method." Our "new critics" have by now nearly succeeded in discrediting that method, and one should go along with them insofar as their motive is to devise a more adequate mode of teaching literature and writing about it. At the same time, however, one is appalled by the intellectual naïveté manifest in their failure to distinguish between creative historical insight (as you find it in such diverse thinkers as Herder, Goethe, Marx, Nietzsche, and Toynbee, or, for that matter, in T. S. Eliot at his empirical best or a fine scholar-critic like Erich Auerbach) and the "historical method" of the old-time professors, whose laborious tracing of sources and mechanical accumulation of historical facts for their own sake is at its best merely a form of documentation, no matter how useful, and at its worst a form of antiquarianism. If the "purpose of historical research is to understand the present," as Mr. Hauser maintains, then the academic researchers in literature evade that task by retreating into the sheer facticity of the past. The "new critics," on the other hand, converge on the literary text, which, after all, regardless of the age it was composed in, is in a sense a piece of irreducible presentness. Their attachment to the text is what is appealing about the "new critics"; what is unappealing is their neglect of context. Only in the medium of historical time is that context to be apprehended; and there is a dialectical relation between text and context, which, if ignored in principle, must eventually lead to the impoverishment of the critical faculty and a devitalized sense of literary art. Thus in the long run the neglect of context is paid for by the increasing misuse and misreading of the text itself. For the historicity of a text is inextricably involved in its nature and function, just as it is involved in the nature and function of language, law, religion, political institutions, etc. Nor is the historicity of a text to be equated with any given series of historical facts. The historical fact is as such no more than a neutral datum, whereas historicity is a value created by the power of the historical imagination.

Nietzsche spoke of the historical sense as a new faculty of the mind, a sixth sense. It is at once an analytic instrument and a bracing resource of the modern sensibility. To confuse it with conventional historical studies is an elementary blunder. It has led the "new critics," particularly the men of the younger academic generation, who appear to be bitten by the spirit of faction and the conceit of up-to-dateness in method, to reject the historical appreciation of literary art, replacing it with a narrow textual-formalistic approach which cannot account for change and movement in literature and which systematically eliminates ideas from criticism: and without ideas it is impossible to connect the literary interest with other interests. Nor is an inflated and abstruse terminology a substitute for ideas. It is mainly for the lack of such connective ideas—which alone enable us to assimilate literature to the historical world at large whence it comes and whither it longs to return—that the "new criticism" has lately exposed itself to the charge of sectarianism and downright tediousness. The complaint is justified, I think, though it scarcely applies to such older critics as Tate, Ransom, and Blackmur, whose virtues and faults are primarily their own; they are intractably their own men, so marked in their individual character and high critical intelligence as not to fit neatly into any school. It is the epigone-like disciples, coming upon the scene too late to have absorbed the exhilarating literary spirit of the twenties, who really make up the school of the "new criticism." And what, at bottom, is that criticism, considered not in the sense of Ransom's book of that title but in the sense of its actual practice during the past decade? It is essentially an amalgam of diluted formalism and diluted traditionalism (Eliot's version of it). I call it an amalgam because its two elements are artificially combined, in a forced congruity. The diluting results from the domestication habitually enforced by the academy.

Where Mr. Hauser comes in after this digression is that his book, like Erich Auerbach's *Mimesis,* so patently offers us at least one instructive alternative to critical sectarianism. The stimulative effect can be gauged by comparing Mr. Hauser's passages on such writers as Balzac and Flaubert with the treatment of them in *The Novel in France,* a recent work by Mr. Martin Turnell, who might be said to belong to the British wing of the "new criticism." Mr. Turnell, attempting to run down both Balzac and Flaubert, judges the former to be a writer of sloppy prose with an immature outlook on life and the latter as perhaps even more immature, a cynic in fact, whose fiction represents "an attack on human nature." To my mind, this attempted revision of the canon of the French novel falls wide of the mark. It draws no support from the historical sensibility. This is not to say that Mr. Turnell is unaware of the factual-historical background of the novelists he has set out to depose. It is rather that the historical dimension of their art escapes him. Hence he is forced back into a tight moralism of judgment; also to disregard the variability of the novelistic gift, which is not an abstract potential but is actualized on the historical plane and is to be perceived on no other plane. Balzac is by now so far removed from us that a response to the historicity of his work is essential to our enjoyment of it. This is less true of Flaubert, who is in a sense still our contemporary; but the contemporaneous too is badly understood when the historical sense is weakly operative.

Mr. Turnell, for example, attributes the faults he discerns in Flaubert to his personal manias. For my part, I find unacceptable this approach to a writer of Flaubert's stature and immensely symbolic significance in modern letters. Mr. Hauser sees quite as clearly as Mr. Turnell the inhumanity of Flaubert's aesthetic fanaticism and his lack of a direct relationship to life. But he also sees something else, something more ambiguous and touching and inevitable: the torment of an artist in whom romanticism had turned so self-conscious and problematical that it compelled him to outrage his own instincts and inclinations, thus enacting a sacrificial role. Certain things had become historically inescapable in Flaubert's time and it is exactly because he chose to take the burden of them upon himself that he is so authentic, so formidable even in his failures. Is his struggle for the *mot juste* merely a

214

personal aberration? It is a sign, Mr. Hauser notes, of the gulf that had opened up in the artistic career between "the 'possession' of life and the 'expression' of it." One thinks of Henry James, whose stylistic distillations of the later period are likewise implicated in this division. James, of course, was not forced to struggle for the *mot juste*. It came to him with an ease as astonishing as it is suspect. For James, unlike the disconsolate Frenchman, finally succeeded only too well in repressing within himself the human hunger for immediacy and spontaneity. His rules of art, i.e., his vaunted aesthetic of the novel, is intrinsically an effort to vindicate the consequent estrangement and to derive from it a discipline of creative work. His triumph was that he achieved that discipline and that even in his state of estrangement he continued to pay homage to the "possession" of life.

Mr. Hauser's long passage on Flaubert is built along the lines of synoptic characterization, the classic resource of criticism. It is a masterful critical-historical *récit*, as are the passages on Rousseau, Richardson, Stendhal, Balzac, Dostoevsky, and Tolstoy. Of *Madame Bovary* he writes:

Flaubert's statement, *"Madame Bovary, c'est moi,"* is true in a double sense. He must often have had the feeling that not merely the romanticism of his youth but also his criticism of romanticism . . . was a life-fantasy. *Madame Bovary* owes its artistic veracity and opportuneness to the intensity with which he experienced the problem of this life-fantasy, the crises of self-deception and the falsification of his own personality. When the meaning of romanticism became problematical, the whole questionableness of modern man was revealed—his escape from the present, his constant desire to be somewhere different from where he has to be . . . because he is afraid of the proximity and responsibility for the present. The analysis of romanticism led to the diagnosis of the disease of the whole century, to the recognition of the neurosis, the victims of which are incapable of giving an account of themselves, and would always prefer to be inside other peoples' skins, not seeing themselves as they really are, but as they would like to be. In this self-deception and falsification of life . . . Flaubert seizes hold of the essence of the modern subjectivism that distorts everything with which it comes in contact. The feeling

215

that we possess only a deformed version of reality and that we are imprisoned in the subjective forms of our thinking is first given full artistic expression in *Madame Bovary*. . . . The transformation of reality by the human consciousness, already pointed out by Kant, acquired in the course of the nineteenth century the character of an alternately more or less conscious and unconscious illusion, and called forth attempts to explain and unmask it, such as historical materialism and psychoanalysis. With his interpretation of romanticism, Flaubert is one of the great revealers and unmaskers of the century, and, therefore, one of the founders of the modern, reflexive outlook on life.

L'Education sentimentale Mr. Hauser analyzes as a novel of which the true hero is time. Time serves in it in a double role, both as "the element which conditions and gives life to the characters" and as the principle by which "they are worn out, destroyed and devoured." It was romanticism which discovered creative, seminal time, while in the reaction against romanticism time was discovered to be a corrupting element, undermining and draining man's life. Thus "this gradual, imperceptible, irresistible pining away, the silent undermining of life, which does not even produce the startling bang of the great, imposing catastrophe, is the experience around which the *Education sentimentale* and practically the whole modern novel revolves"—an experience non-tragic and undramatic and therefore appropriately cast in the narrative mode. Here we have a key to the dominant position of the novel in the modern age. It is the medium which lends itself more easily than the play or the poem to the representation of life in its mechanized, commonplace, and frustrating aspects, and of time as a destructive force. The novel develops its formal principle from this idea of the corrosive effects of time, just as tragedy derives "the basis of its form from the idea of the timeless fate which destroys man with one fell blow. And as fate possesses a superhuman greatness and a metaphysical power in tragedy, so time attains an inordinate, almost mythical dimension in the novel."

This analysis of the time-experience of the present age is developed in the last chapter with greater complexity and absorption in detail. Time has for contemporary man a quality of immediateness such as it could never have had in the past. Modern technics have made him conscious of "the contiguity, the interconnections and dovetailing of things and processes," with the result that he has become fascinated by "simultaneity," which is a kind of universalism of the temporal dimension. Not only the cinema, the medium most naturally adapted to produce effects of "simultaneity," but modern art as a whole reaches out for this same magical illusionism of time, borrowing from the cinema whatever it can. Mr. Hauser sees this Bergsonian *simultanéité des états d'âmes* as the basic experience of painting, for instance, connecting its multiform tendencies, the futurism of the Italians with the expressionism of Chagall, the cubism of Picasso with the surrealism of Chirico, Ernst, and Dali. The film Mr. Hauser evaluates as a form that accommodates itself above all to the analysis of time, capable of representing visually those processes which previously only music could express. But the film is still an empty form, whose "real life has not yet arrived." In the meantime the novel has appropriated some of its techniques. Thus "the discontinuity of the plot and the scenic development, the sudden emersion of the thoughts and moods, the relativity and the inconsistency of the time-standards, are what remind us in the works of Proust and Joyce, Dos Passos and Virginia Woolf of the cutting, dissolves and interpolations of the film, and it is simply film-magic when Proust brings two incidents, which may lie thirty years before, as closely together as if there were only two hours between them." Joyce is even more radical in his effort to free time of its chronological articulation; and one may add the poetry of Pound and Eliot as further examples. But what is the meaning of this intermingling of past and present across the boundaries of space and time? "Simultaneity" is hardly an end in itself. In height-

217

ening our sense of time it also induces in us the feeling that all our experiences occur at one and the same time. Thus the ultimate effect is that of the negation of time—a negation implying an effort for the recovery of that inwardness for which we long in the midst of our chaotic modernity.

Mr. Hauser evaluates writers and painters almost entirely by indirection, through a phenomenological description and analysis of the worlds they wrested from chaos. He does not share the predilection of contemporary Anglo-American criticism for the outright "ranking" of artists in a strictly graded hierarchy of achievement. I have sometimes wondered whether this passion for "ranking," for establishing with an almost obsessive conscientiousness the exact degree of one writer's alleged superiority to another and his precise place in the hierarchy, does not actually mask an inner uncertainty and even skepticism as to the value of art altogether? A skepticism so threatening would naturally seek compensation in ideas and procedures of a diametrically opposite order, such as the fetishism of art and the urge to control the imaginative process by setting up fixed and conclusive standards that are good for all time and thus serve as a barrier to the nihilism of the age, which affects everything and everybody, including the hierophants of art and culture. Mr. Hauser's historicism enables him to resist the temptation to idolize the art-object and to overestimate its saving power. But his approach is not immune to the relativization of value inherent in historicism. The peril is real, and his endeavor is to save himself by plunging into the reality of history as into a restorative medium. While not going so far as Ortega y Gasset, who has put forth the claim that man has no nature but only a history, nevertheless his practice throughout is to grasp all ideas and ideals by disclosing their historical import, which thus becomes the main guaranty of their actuality.

The expository mode he adopts is that of the polyphonic organization of historical themes, enormously varied in their bearing and significance, dealt with not summarily but with extraordinary informedness and wide-ranging scholarship, taking in all major art-movements and coming to rest in the extended consideration of single figures who might be said to sum up their time or to initiate the transition to a new epoch. And at all points he is concerned with determining the public status of the artist in any given period, the social value attached to the phenomenon of art, the meaning of the idea of artistic freedom and autonomy, and the evolution of the concept of genius. This latter concept is so familiar to us that we tend to project it backward into past ages, ascribing a permanence to it which it wholly lacks, since it is thoroughly imbued with historical motives. It was foreign to the Middle Ages, whose superpersonal, objective, and authoritarian culture allowed for no strong sense of intellectual property and individual originality. The basic change occurs in the Renaissance, when famous masters like Michelangelo, Raphael, and Titian begin to outshine their patrons, becoming great lords themselves. Mr. Hauser perceives in Michelangelo "the first example of the modern, lonely, demoniacally impelled artist . . . who feels a deep sense of responsibility toward his gifts and sees a higher and superhuman power in his own artistic genius." Genius, both as cult and idea, is a fundamentally new element in the valuation of art; implicit in it is the notion that "the work of art is the creation of an autocratic personality, that this personality transcends tradition, theory and rules, even the work itself, being richer and deeper than the work and impossible to express adequately within any objective form." From this notion it is but a step—though the Renaissance never made this step—to the notion of the misunderstood genius and the appeal to posterity against the verdict of the contemporary world. The idea of the autonomy of art parallels the idea of genius, for it gives expression in an objective manner, that is from the standpoint of the work, to what is expressed subjectively, from the stand-

219

point of the artist, in his claim to be a uniquely creative person. But there is far more content than that in the idea of the autonomy of art. Indeed, I am conscious of simplifying Mr. Hauser's exploration of this and other themes, which take him into shifts and modulations of meaning that depend on elaborate excursions into social and economic history. His method enforces the constant recourse to the means of analysis furnished by sociology and psychology, and the use of such means are indispensable to the fulfillment of his purpose. There are certain problems and attitudes in art, not open to the direct "intrinsic" approach, which become accessible through the detour of the approach from without. An instance of this sort of problem is aestheticism, more specifically the attitude of *l'art pour l'art,* which Mr. Hauser interprets as being "partly the expression of the division of labor which advances hand in hand with industrialization, and partly the bulwark of art against the danger of being swallowed up by industrialized and mechanized life. It signifies, on the one hand, the rationalization, disenchantment and contraction of art, but simultaneously the attempt to preserve its individual quality and spontaneity, in spite of the universal mechanization of life."

Mr. Hauser is quite aware of the limitations of his method. He knows very well that artistic quality cannot be explained sociologically, nor does he offer such explanations. And time and again he asserts that artistic progress—in the sense of movement, change, and innovation—is frequently compatible with political conservatism, that not only is there no direct relation between progressiveness in art and conservatism in politics but that they are indeed "incommensurable in the two spheres." What is important is the artist's sincerity and fidelity to his vision of life, which sufficiently account for his enlightening influence on his age. There is, however, a complication in the idea of "compatibility," as exemplified in the case of novelists like Balzac and Dostoevsky. Not a few works of art display an internal

220

antagonism between their material and spiritual qualities or an antithesis between their latent and manifest content: hence the contradiction which is sometimes to be observed between a writer's proclaimed ideology and the inner meaning of his imaginative creations. For instance, the first generation of French romantic writers were to begin with legitimists and clericalists while at the same time assaulting with might and main the conservative classical tradition in literature, which was then defended mainly by the liberals; a more modern instance are certain poets of traditionalist bias in whom a genuine aesthetic liberalism and openness toward the future goes hand in hand with historical reaction. Neither in art nor in life is there a pre-established harmony guaranteeing the even and unified development of all the elements that combine to form objects of value. Advance in one sphere is often paid for by regression in another.

The literature of the modern period is particularly exposed, I would say, to inner antagonisms and contradictions. Critics who are perturbed by these contradictions, preferring the writers they deal with to be of one mind, are prone to expend much ingenious cerebration in inventing unified creative personalities where none perhaps exists. They would do better to try getting at a writer's truth by fathoming the depth and intensity of the contradiction of which he is the carrier and which more often than not proves to be the wayward secret of his power over us. Fortunately, literature is not a function of criticism, no matter how methodologically refined or overbearingly intent on moral suasion. It makes its own arrangements with life, and its victories and defeats are also its own.

1952

X. AMERICAN INTELLECTUALS

IN THE POSTWAR SITUATION*

It is true of course that of late American artists and
intellectuals have largely come to terms with the realities of the national life. Hence, if they no longer feel
"disinherited" and "astray" neither for that matter are
they attached any longer to the attitudes of dissidence and
revolt that prevailed among them for some decades. As
their mood has gradually shifted from opposition to
acceptance, they have grown unreceptive to extreme
ideas, less exacting and "pure" in ideological commitment, more open to the persuasions of actuality. This far-
reaching change has by no means run its course. It is of a
complexity not to be grasped by a simple approach,
whether positive or negative; and it is easy to fall into
one-sided constructions in discussing it.

Among the factors entering into the change, the principal one, to my mind, is the exposure of the Soviet myth
and the consequent resolve (shared by nearly all but the
few remaining fellow-travelers) to be done with Utopian illusions and heady expectations. In their chastened
mood American democracy looks like the real thing to
the intellectuals. Its incontestable virtue is that, for all its

* A contribution to the *Partisan Review* symposium, "Our
Country and Our Culture," May-June 1952

distortions and contradictions, it actually exists. It is not a mere theory or a deduction from some textbook in world-salvation. Whether capitalist or not, it has so far sustained that freedom of expression and experiment without which the survival of the intelligence is inconceivable in a modern society—a society lacking any organic basis, social or religious, for unity of belief or uniformity of conduct. In the palmy days when it was possible to take democracy for granted—that is, before the rise to global power of Hitlerism and then of Stalinism—the intellectuals were hardly aware of the very tangible benefits they derived from it. Now, however, only the most doctrinaire types would be disposed to trade in those benefits for some imaginary perfection of good in the remote future.

This change of perspective has inevitably made for a greater degree of identification with American life, with its traditions and prospects; and to suppose that this is simply a regression to nationalism is a mistake. (The nationalist motive is in fact far more strongly operative among European than among American intellectuals.) What has happened, rather, is that we have gained a sense of immediate relatedness to the national environment, a sense of what is concretely even if minimally our own. In these terms one can indeed speak of a 'reconciliation' of the intellectuals.

Another factor, relating to the arts proper, is that the passage of time has considerably blunted the edge of the old Jamesian complaint as to the barrenness of the native scene. James was surely right in drawing the moral that "the flower of art blooms only where the soil is deep, that it takes a great deal of history to produce a little literature, that it needs a complex social machinery to set a writer in motion." But since 1879, when that severe sentence was written, much has happened to modify the conditions James deplored. For one thing, the time is past when "business alone was respectable" in America and when many of its artists were therefore forced into

223

a state of dreary and dreamy isolation. The businessman, though still a most formidable figure, is no longer looked up to as the one and only culture-hero of the country: not since the debacle of 1929, at any rate. Moreover, the national literature has now accumulated a substantial tradition and the dynamism of our historical life in this century has brought into existence a social machinery more than sufficiently complex for literary purposes. This is not to say that this machinery works beneficently; there is no necessary relation between beneficence and literary purpose. If anything, the machinery has now become so prodigious, so vast in operation and prodigal in performance, that the writer is just as likely to be thrown back as to be set into motion by it.

As for the Jamesian vision of Europe as the "rich, deep, dark Old World," its appeal has been markedly reduced by a series of social upheavals, revolutions, and two world wars. The historical richness is still there, though what it comes to at present is hardly more than a combination of décor and recollection; it is the depths and the darkness of the Old World that are almost intolerably actual at present, and in that oppressive atmosphere the Jamesian vision pales and dissolves. It is hard to believe that western Europe has lost its cultural priority for good, even if for the time being the social and political strains are too great to permit the exercise of leadership. Its past is not in question here, since we cannot but appropriate it as our past too. What is in question is the effort of comtemporaries, and that effort is of a scale and intensity insufficient to compel our attention or to provoke meaningful reactions in American culture. Existentialism was, I suppose, the last consequential movement to engage our interest, but the literary work that it produced turned out to be of small consequence. Moreover, the impression is that much of the culture-building energy of Europe's intellectuals is now dissipated in political adventurism; that in their thinking both of their position and ours they are apt to fall into disastrous oversimplifications, such as putting the United States and the Soviet Empire on the same level as rival power-blocs, and that far too many are tempted to be done with it all by plunging into the abyss of Stalin's Utopia.

But if among us that fatal temptation has been largely overcome, it is scarcely because we have been especially endowed with good sense or idealism. The difference lies in the more fortunate, more spacious American environment. Thus it is imperative not to overlook so direct and concrete a factor as the long spell of prosperity that America has enjoyed since the War. It has at long last effected the absorption of the intellectuals into the institutional life of the country. The prosperity that followed the First World War had no such result, the game being strictly business and the intellectuals remaining mostly on the outside looking in, while this time their status has been strikingly improved by the phenomenal expansion of the economy. Writers and artists have succeeded in breaking down the scholastic barriers that kept them out of university teaching, and many economists and sociologists have made their way into government bureaus. In particular it has been the many-sided extension of the educational system which has furnished the greater opportunity. Consider that the intellectual bohemian or proletarian has turned into a marginal figure nowadays, reminding us in his rather quixotic aloneness of the ardors and truancies of the past. We are witnessing a process that might well be described as that of the *embourgeoisement* of the American intelligentsia—a process that is plainly not unconnected with the changes of mind and mood we are analyzing in this symposium. In the main, it accounts for the fact that the idea of socialism, whether in its revolutionary or democratic reference, has virtually ceased to figure in current intellectual discussion.

Yet the material security so newly gained must be seen as an achievement of the American system not under

225

normal conditions but under the stress of war and preparation for war. We have been drawn, as Reinhold Niebuhr recently put it, into "an historic situation in which the paradise of our domestic security is suspended in a hell of global insecurity." "Suspended" is the key word, for a good many other satisfactions of American life similarly exist in a state of insecure suspension. The fact is that the cold war has reduced social tensions within the nation even as it has increased international tension. The war-geared economy has made for conditions of prosperity which again are typically taken to mean that "good Americanism" contains within itself the secret of overcoming the hazards of history. The illusion that our society is in its very nature immune to tragic social conflicts and collisions has been revived, and once more it is assumed that the more acute problems of the modern epoch are unreal so far as we are concerned. And in their recoil from radicalism certain intellectuals have now made that easy assumption their own. Not that they say so openly, but their complacence and spiritual torpor quite give them away.

Especially vulnerable in this respect are some of the ex-radicals and ex-Marxists, who have gone so far in smoothly re-adapting themselves, in unlearning the old and learning the new lessons, as to be scarcely distinguishable from the common run of philistines. In their narrow world anti-Stalinism has become almost a professional stance. It has come to mean so much that it excludes nearly all other concerns and ideas, with the result that they are trying to turn anti-Stalinism into something which it can never be: a total outlook on life, no less, or even a philosophy of history. Apparently some of them find it altogether easy to put up with the vicious antics of a political bum like Senator McCarthy, even as they grow more and more intolerant of any basic criticism of existing social arrangements.

The old anti-Stalinism of the independent Left had the true pathos and conviction of a minority fighting under its own banner for its own ends; but that was back in the thirties and early forties. Its function then was to warn—and though the warning was not heeded the anti-Stalinists of that period played a vanguard role in that they were the first to discern the totalitarian essence of the Soviet myth. Since then, however, that minority political grouping has lost its bearings, continuing to denounce the evils of Communism with deadly sameness and in apparent obliviousness of the fact that in the past few years anti-Stalinism has virtually become the official creed of our entire society. What is needed is not more and more demonstrations of the badness of Stalinism but some workable ideas as to how to go about preparing its defeat. The locus of political action has shifted to the sphere of foreign policy, and it is precisely in the formulation and discussion of foreign policy that the deconverted radicals, with very few exceptions, have displayed no special aptitude or initiative or grasp of the immensely perplexing problems that will have to be solved before American leadership of the free world can be made to yield positive results.*

* Characteristic of the petrified anti-Stalinists is their inability to distinguish between Communism as an external and as an internal danger. For Communism, though surely a grave danger *to* America—perhaps the gravest that the nation has had to cope with since the Civil War—is hardly so grave a danger *in* America. The local Party has lost its power in the trade unions, it has been deserted by nearly half its membership, and it has only a residual hold on some sections of liberal opinion. The Kremlin's postwar strategy has all but destroyed the influence of the American Communists, an influence almost wholly due to their success in deceiving people as to their real allegiance and intention. In the period of the People's Front and later of the war-alliance with Russia, conditions were extremely favorable to the Stalinist strategy of deception and infiltration. These conditions no longer exist in this country, and the nation as a whole has now been able to take the measure of the party-liners and their assorted dupes and stooges. No doubt they still have a nuisance value to the Kremlin, but to regard them on that account as the main danger *inside* the U.S. is to escape from actualities into the

227

"It is difficult to change gods," says Shatov to Stavrogin in *The Possessed*. Shatov, who turns from "nihilism" to orthodoxy and national messianism, knows whereof he is speaking. One wishes that more people among us confessed to the difficulty, instead of engaging themselves with unseemly haste to positions so safe and sound as to be devoid of all moral or intellectual content. There is the emergent group of parvenu conservatives, for instance, who, having but lately discovered the pleasures of conformity, are now aggressively bent on combating all dissent from the bourgeois outlook and devaluating the critical traditions of modern thought. Thus it has become fashionable to dismiss ideas of cultural or social insurgence by relating them, with a facility all too suspect, to the Russian experience, while at the same time all sorts of heretofore unsuspected plausibilities—if not profundities—are read into the standard notions of the ideologues of reaction; and a new magazine like *The Freeman,* with its boosting of laissez faire and hero-worship of Taft and McCarthy, is by no means an untypical phenomenon.

In our literary culture there is a more complicated play of forces. The rout of the left-wing movement has depoliticalized literature—which is not necessarily a bad thing in itself if the political motive had been not simply abandoned but creatively displaced by a root-idea of a different order. No such idea has emerged so far; what is to be observed now is a kind of detachment from principle and fragmentation of the literary life. Also to

shadow-world of political sectarianism and sheer obsession. Of course, so long as the Soviet power exists its propagandists and spies will circulate among us, and it is up to the intelligence agencies of the government to deal with them. It is scarcely the function of political-minded intellectuals, however, to serve as an adjunct to the F.B.I. The necessity of continuing and widening the ideological struggle against Communism on a world scale goes without saying; but in order to succeed that struggle must be conducted with more enlightened assumptions and with positive ends in view.

be observed is the rise of a neo-philistine tendency, an oddly belated growth of the mood of acceptance and of the defensive reaction to Communism, which, if unchecked by the revival of the critical spirit, threatens to submerge the tradition of dissent in American writing.

The neo-philistines make an opportune kind of optimism their credo; they are impatient to assume the unchallengeable reality of the "world," and while reconciled to mass-culture they are inclined to deprecate the traditional attitudes of the literary and artistic avant-garde—attitudes said to arise out of negativism pure and simple and willful indulgence in "alienation." Now the avant-garde is of course open to criticism. It has the typical faults of its incongruous position in a mass-society, such as snobbery and pride of caste. It is disposed to take a much too solemn and devotional view of the artist's vocation. Its distortions of perspective result from its aloofness and somewhat inflexible morality of opposition. But to accuse it of having invented alienation is ludicrous. For what the avant-garde actually represents historically, from its very beginnings in the early nineteenth century, is the effort to preserve the integrity of art and the intellect amidst the conditions of alienation brought on by the major social forces of the modern era. The avant-garde has attempted to ward off the ravages of alienation in a number of ways: by means of developing a tradition of its own and cultivating its own group norms and standards, by resisting the bourgeois incentives to accommodation and perforce making a virtue of its separateness from the mass. That this strategy has in the main been successful is demonstrated by the only test that really counts—the test of creative achievement. After all, it is chiefly the avant-garde which must be given credit for the production of most of the literary masterpieces of the past hundred years, from *Madame Bovary* to the *Four Quartets;* and the other arts are equally indebted to its venturesome spirit.

If the artists of the avant-garde are alienated, as it is

said, then at least they are free to convert their consciousness of that unhappy state into an imaginative resource. This cannot be claimed for the artists in mass-culture, whose function literally depends on their capacity to cultivate a kind of strategic unawareness of meaning and consequence. Of course, there are certain elements in mass-culture, some types of jazz and the folklore of sport for instance, that have a positive value. On the whole, though, the proliferation of kitsch in this country under the leveling stimulus of the profit-motive is a liability of our society which is not to be wished away by pious appeals to democracy and the rights of the "common man." But if under present conditions we cannot stop the ruthless expansion of mass-culture, the least we can do is to keep apart and refuse its favors.

1952

XI. THE EDUCATION OF
ANTON CHEKHOV

The understanding of Chekhov's background and personality is greatly enhanced by a reading of his *Selected Letters*, edited by Lillian Hellman and translated by Sidonie K. Lederer. From first to last the impression conveyed is that of astounding courage and of heroic manliness and self-possession. Dead at the age of forty-four, apparently Chekhov knew well enough even before reaching his mid-twenties that his life would be short and racked with hurt and pain; and he resolutely kept that knowledge from his family and friends. The severe and repeated pulmonary hemorrhages and other afflictions he suffered would surely have laid low anyone more self-indulgent or open to the not inconsiderable spiritual temptations of disease and physical debility. Another exacerbating circumstance was the material pressure he was under since early youth when he had first undertaken the major responsibility for the support of his large family, mostly made up of weaklings and ne'er-do-wells. All in all he had little time for imaginative self-realization, and a good part of the time he did have was consumed in the study and practice of medicine as well as in the frequent travels and changes of abode forced upon him by the state of his health.

Thus what comes through to us most vividly in his letters is a sense of the enormous odds against which Chekhov pitted himself in striving to achieve those rare qualities of his narrative and dramatic art that make it so uniquely his own. This art is at once astringent and poetic, circumstantially exact in a prose-sense yet structurally allied to the lyric mode. It is an art of unmistakable originality though not of the very first order; and if it is known above all for fixing imperishably conditions of human staleness, futility, torpor, and ennui, the explanation is not to be sought in any hidden enervation of the author or covert sympathy for negative states of being—he was no Baudelairean bell with a crack in it— but rather in the passionate even if undemonstrative integrity with which he resisted the denial of life's richer and finer possibilities.

A late child of the fatally belated Russian Enlightenment and the last important figure in the great nineteenth-century line of the masters of Russian prose, he believed that life could be lived with intelligence and love, without coercion and falsehood, at the same time that he concentrated on showing that life as actually lived was sad and boring. But in his expression of this sadness and boredom there is no finality (of acceptance or complicity or mean pleasure in exposure and reduction), such as we find in many similar evocations of negative states in Western literature of the modern period. The petty decadence inherent in such evocations is entirely alien to Chekhov. He is not attacking human nature, saying that this is the way things are and always will be, while calling for some impossible transcendence which is no more than a metaphysical coda to positive despair. The pessimism commonly ascribed to him is one of mood and temperament perhaps, and it no doubt reflects the stalemate reached by Russian society at the time of his emergence on the literary scene; but it never is a pessimism of ultimate belief and vision. The voice that cries out "No, one cannot go on living like

232

that!" at the end of one of his typical anecdotes of wasted existence ("The Man in a Shell") is indubitably that of the writer; and in that somber masterpiece "Ward No. 6" he identifies himself most lucidly and credibly with the standpoint of the madman Gromov, whose madness is of a piece with his refusal to come to terms with "human baseness and oppression trampling up truth" and to renounce his faith that "a splendid life will in time prevail upon the earth." The source of the powerful emotion embodied in this tale is the felt idea that however forlorn the world of men may be it nevertheless contains within itself the promise of release and change. It is the wonder and triumph of Chekhov that the animating principle of his pathos of "lives clipped and wingless" is resistance to slackness and inertia—the seepage of the psyche epitomized in the term Oblomovism. Let us keep in mind, though, that only one form of Oblomovism is represented in Goncharov's famous novel. Chekhov's insight penetrated to other and more complicated forms of it that are perhaps not so easily determinable; and Oblomovism, after all, is a state not merely of Russia but of the soul.

These letters, if read in conjunction with any fairly adequate biography, enforce the conviction of a productive life whose end is for once not in its beginnings but is marked throughout by change, growth, increasing self-development and self-mastery, *Bildung* and *Selbstbildung* in the classic sense. It can justly be said of Chekhov that the sum of what happened to him is that he achieved an education toward freedom. "The sense of personal freedom," he wrote, "is the chief constituent of creative genius," and the freedom he thus invokes is scarcely to be understood without reference to his beginnings, his ancestry, his childhood, the formative years. The grandson of a serf and the son of a petty tradesman, he suffered in his childhood and early youth the ravages of that backwardness, cruelty, and servility which were as much a family as a national inheritance. If all his life he remained immune to the appeal of the Russian ver-

233

sions of traditionalism, if he remained an agnostic and a radical, a resolute friend of the West and advocate of science and the secular intelligence, it is largely because of the lessons absorbed in those formative years. It is with irresistible concreteness that he put his case to a correspondent: "From childhood I have believed in progress and cannot help believing, as the difference between the time when I got whipped and the time when the whippings ceased was terrific."

The perception of this difference is ineluctably one of the great points of the arduous educational process through which he strove to attain his freedom. He literally had to make himself over to undo the stultification brought on by the early influences that played upon him, influences in no way fortuitous but imbedded in Russian life. In this respect the *locus classicus,* from the standpoint of the biographer and the literary critic alike, is the passage in his letter to Suvorin of January 7, 1889, in which he explains why plebeian writers must buy at the price of their youth what the writers of the gentry have been endowed with by nature. "Go ahead," he tells Suvorin, "and write a story about a young man, the son of a serf, an ex-small shopkeeper, a choir boy, high school and university student, brought up on respect for rank, kissing priests' hands, and the worship of others' ideas, offering thanks for every mouthful of bread, often whipped, going to school without shoes, fighting, torturing animals, fond of dining with rich relatives, playing the hypocrite before God and people without any cause, except that of a consciousness of his own insignificance —then tell how this young man squeezes the slave out of himself one drop at a time and how he wakes one fine morning to feel that in his veins flows not the blood of a slave but real human blood. . . ." Here we come upon the essence of Chekhov's story and upon the basic Chekhovian theme. In this effort to squeeze the slave out of himself we confront the actuality of his education, the ordeal of it, the struggle, the relapses, the price paid

234

and the victory scored. The meaning of this education, in the sense of its absolute necessity and the consequences of failure to undertake it, forms the sum and substance of the criticism of life contained in his plays and fictions.

Chekhov was intrinsically too modest in his spiritual make-up and too much of a wry realist (no wonder he objected to Dostoevsky's novels on the ground of their "immodesty") to be capable of engaging in momentous affirmations carrying him beyond the experience provided by his time and environment. For this and related reasons it is far from difficult to make out, as some commentators have done, that generally all he leaves us with is a mood of "delicious depression." Such a view is wholly erroneous, to my mind. We cannot gain anything like a full recovery of the import of his work unless we grasp the one surpassing moral intuition controlling it —that man can hope to realize the promise of his humanity only if he succeeds in overcoming the slave within himself in all his guises and disguises. The Rilkean dictum "You must change your life!" is implicit in the entire Chekhovian statement. But to interpret this one fundamental intuition in a bare political sense, as the Soviet critics are instructing their readers to do to the benefit of the official dogma, is patently a gross oversimplification. A slave is not transformed into a man by changing masters. Moreover, the slave in man is a cunning animal that knows not only how to survive changes, however radical, in social institutions but also how to adapt such changes to suit his nature. "People must never be humiliated—that is the main thing," Chekhov wrote in an early letter; and in a later one he wrote: "God's earth is good. It is only we on it who are bad. . . . The important thing is that we must be just, and all the rest will be added unto us." It is in the light of such precepts that he is best understood. To take him simply as a critic of Russian society at a certain stage of its development is to limit him intolerably.

In one of her engaging and perceptive introductory notes to the text of this volume, Miss Hellman remarks that Chekhov was without "that final spiritual violence which the very great creative artist has always had. And he knew it as he knew most things about himself." To this I would assent, though with some uneasiness about the use of the word violence as the clincher in her formulation. Ultimate imaginative power need not necessarily be equated with the shock tactics of frenzied and eruptive geniuses. One agrees, none the less, that such ultimate power is wanting in Chekhov. Perhaps the crux of the matter is that he expended so much vitality on his exemplary education that what was left could not suffice to carry him beyond the lessons that engrossed him. This too is of course among the lessons he learned, as is implied in his rueful saying that he was forced to buy at the price of his youth what others are endowed with by nature. He was certainly aware that he never really got all he bargained for. Still, taking everything into account, the stricken life and the fashioned work, the price was well worth paying. For his effort to redeem the age he lived in he deserves to be ranked as nearly the equal of his great predecessors in Russian letters.

1955

INDEX

NEW DIRECTIONS PAPERBOOKS